'A Coronation, in the mere character of a national
spectacle, serious as well as splendid, bears with it a degree of natural
curiosity; but there are points interwoven with the solemnity which ought
rather to demand attention to consider, than excite anxiety to behold.'[1]

T.C. Banks, *An Historical and Critical Enquiry into the
Nature of the Kingly Office*, 1814

FOLLOWING PAGE
Queen Elizabeth II and the Duke of Edinburgh returning to Buckingham Palace
after the Coronation, June 2 1953.

CORONATION

The Crowning of Elizabeth II

Hugo Vickers

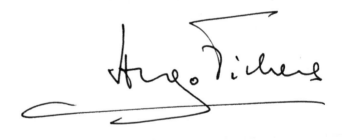

THE DOVECOTE PRESS

To Arthur, George and Alice, with love from their father.

First published in 2013
This new revised edition first published in February 2023
by The Dovecote Press Ltd
Marshwood, Bridport, Dorset DT6 5QL

ISBN 978-0-9573119-6-1
Text © Hugo Vickers 2013 & 2023
Illustrations by Osbert Lancaster © National Library of Scotland
Illustration by Cecil Beaton © National Portrait Gallery, London
All other illustrations – private collection

Hugo Vickers has asserted his rights under the Copyright, Designs
and Patent Act 1988 to be identified as author of this work

Designed by The Dovecote Press
Printed and bound by T J Books, Cornwall

All papers used by The Dovecote Press are natural,
recyclable products made from wood grown in sustainable,
well-managed forests

A CIP catalogue record for this book is available
from the British Library

Contents

Introduction

Queen Elizabeth II in Windsor 2022

photograph © Gill Heppell

INTRODUCTION

Queen Elizabeth II celebrated the Platinum Jubilee of her reign in 2022. Already in frail health, she made an appearance on the balcony of Buckingham Palace after the Birthday Parade and that evening at Windsor Castle she lit the first of the Jubilee bonfires. Then on the Sunday, at the last minute, she made the further effort to travel from Windsor Castle to appear before the crowds at the end of the Jubilee Pageant. She missed the Thanksgiving Service at St Paul's Cathedral on the Friday morning. Thereafter her public appearances were limited though she was very much in the public eye on her visit to Edinburgh at the end of June. She stayed mainly at Windsor Castle and rode her pony, Emma, in the castle riding school on 18 July, for the last time.

The Queen flew to Scotland for her summer holiday on 21 July. She stayed first at Craigowan Lodge and then moved into Balmoral Castle on 9 August. During those weeks members of her family came to stay as usual. On 6 September she received Boris Johnson in audience as he stepped down as Prime Minister and minutes later she welcomed Liz Truss as her 15th Prime Minister. With a certain symmetry, the first thing she had done on stepping down from the airliner from Kenya in February 1952 was to shake the hand of Winston Churchill, her first Prime Minister, a man born in 1874, while her last constitutional duty was to shake the hand of her last Prime Minister, Liz Truss, who was born in 1975. The following night she cancelled a Privy Council zoom and on the next day, 8 September 2022 she died peacefully at 3.10 pm.

At that moment Prince Charles automatically became King, and the process of confirming him seamlessly in his new role began to unfold. On 10 September he attended the Accession Council at St James's Palace, after which he was proclaimed King across the land. As the Queen's coffin made its progress from Scotland to London and in due course to Windsor, so he went to Westminster Hall and attended parliaments in Scotland, Northern Ireland and Wales.

On 11 October it was announced that his Coronation would take place on 6 May 2023. The statement read:

> Buckingham Palace is pleased to announce that the Coronation of His Majesty The King will take place on Saturday 6th May, 2023. The Coronation Ceremony will take place at Westminster Abbey, London, and will be conducted by the Archbishop of Canterbury. The Ceremony will see His Majesty King Charles III crowned alongside The Queen Consort. The Coronation will reflect the monarch's role today and look towards the future, while being rooted in longstanding traditions and pageantry.

At the time of writing, there has been no formal Proclamation with Heralds in attendance and we have few details of the plans. This book looks at what happened at the Coronation in 1953. Some of the details remain unaltered, being part of the established ritual, but it is already stated that the service will be shorter, that there will be less guests in the Abbey, and a number of obsolete traditions will be dropped. The King said he wanted a modest Coronation, but we want a splendid one, showcasing Britain to the world.

It is likely that the ritual will be carried out with full and traditional splendour, while those invited to be present in Westminster Abbey will represent national diversity.

The Coronation contains a communion service, the purpose of which is to confirm the King as Supreme Governor of the Church of England and this embraces not only the King but everyone present in the Abbey.

Accession

GOD SAVE THE QUEEN!

Shortly after 12.30 on a wet morning on 2 June 1953, the Archbishop of Canterbury raised St Edward's Crown high above the head of the young Queen Elizabeth II, seated in King Edward's Chair. The Queen Mother and young Prince Charles, the Royal Family, the peers and peeresses of the realm, the foreign dignitaries, the Prime Minister and the Commonwealth representatives all waited and watched. The great Abbey went silent. Television viewers monitored the flickering black and white images on tiny screens in their front rooms.

The Archbishop held the crown aloft for a moment and then lowered it onto the Queen's head, placing it first on the forehead and then pressing it down at the back. He then raised his arms high with a little flourish, his prime duty fulfilled.

A great cry went up: 'God Save the Queen!' The peers of the realm put on their coronets in unison, and at the same time a sea of white-gloved arms rose like the necks of swans as the peeresses did likewise. The Abbey resounded with fanfares and loud shouts of acclaim. And through the medium of television and wireless this moment was shared by millions of viewers and listeners, and later seen in all corners of the globe. It can be seen still today, some seventy years later.

This was the culmination of months of meticulous preparation in which every detail of the service had been minutely rehearsed. Ever since the death of King George VI in February 1952, the Earl Marshal (the Duke of Norfolk), the

Archbishop of Canterbury (Dr Geoffrey Fisher) and the Dean of Westminster (Very Rev Alan Don) had been planning the various parts of the service. The Cabinet had been making decisions, the Foreign Office had been wrestling with problems of protocol and precedence. Peers had petitioned by dint of ancient rite to play special parts in the ceremony. Famous figures from the Second World War had been appointed to the great offices of state, some for just that day and no more. Carriages had been spruced up and in some cases borrowed from film studios, troops had been marched through their paces, choristers had been rehearsed, nothing had been left to chance. Every detail had been discussed – down to whether 'the people' in the service sheet should have a capital 'P'.

Coronations had not always run smoothly in the past. Elizabeth I had complained that the holy oil used at her anointing was 'grease, and smelt ill.' At Charles I's service, the left wing of the dove on that particular sceptre broke, which many thought presaged his untimely end. There was a small tremor during James I's coronation which caused some peeresses to faint and terrified the choirboys.

They failed to alter the crown for James II so that it wobbled on his head until Henry Sidney stepped forward to steady it, saying: 'It is not the first time, Sire, that my family has supported the crown.' William and Mary were so different in size, he tall and she short, that they could not balance the sword as they carried it to the altar. The King had no money for the collection until an irritated Lord Danby stepped forward to produce 20 guineas, complaining in a loud voice as he did so.

Queen Anne suffered so badly from gout that she had to be carried to the coronation chair muttering 'my legs may be weak, but head is strong.' George I understood no English and the then Archbishop's German was so poor that that part of the service was translated into 'dog Latin' as they went along. George II became bored at his and was seen winking at a peeress.

George III's Coronation in 1761 was described as 'an affair of muddle, magnificence and odd buffoonery.'[2] The regalia were placed on the table in the wrong order, the sermon was drowned out by the sound of knives and forks as members of the congregation helped themselves to something to eat. Queen

Charlotte had a retiring chamber but was not pleased to find it occupied by the Duke of Newcastle. Then the great diamond fell from the crown on the way out of the Abbey and clattered to the floor.[3] As he reached the Great West Door, the King rebuked the Earl Marshal for his bungling. The Earl Marshal confessed: 'there had been great neglect in that office, but he had now taken such care of registering directions that the *next Coronation* would be conducted with the greatest order imaginable.'[4]

George IV stirred up trouble many years before his coronation by declaring that he had 'a fixed and unalterable determination not to meet the princess of Wales upon any occasion, either in public or private.'[5] Writing in advance of the King's coronation, T.C. Banks, worried that 'the royal ceremonies, of almost eight hundred years national prevalence and custom, will be resolved into the *sic volo, sic jubeo,* of *a new precedent* – !!!'[6] When the time came in 1821, Queen Caroline was famously barred from entering Westminster Abbey.

At his coronation George IV was so hot that he perspired under his robes and mopped his brow with a succession of handkerchiefs. These he handed to the Archbishop of Canterbury who consigned them to the Bishop of Salisbury. 'Several times he was at the last gasp,' noted Lady Cowper. 'He looked more like the victim than the hero of the fête.'[7] He resorted to smelling salts and when he retired to a side aisle, he shook off his clothes and refused to put them on again until he had cooled down.

In 1838 at Queen Victoria's service, the choirboys had been moved from the organ loft to a gallery on the south side. *The Times* correspondent wrote: 'It might have been as well had they been banished entirely from the Abbey, for a more murderous scream of recognition than that which they gave Queen Victoria yesterday was never before heard by civilized ears.'[8]

At the homage, the 87-year-old Lord Rolle fell and rolled down the steps. The Queen advanced and gave him her hand. Towards the end of the service, the Bishop of Bath and Wells turned over two pages of the service at once. The young Queen had retired but had to come out again. At one point she found it all such a muddle that she turned to the Dean of Westminster and asked: 'Pray tell me what I am to do, for they don't know.'[9]

Edward VII had to rescue the crown before it fell, seizing it from the hands of the feeble Archbishop Temple. After doing homage, the Archbishop could not rise and again the King helped him. At the end of the service he collapsed completely, bewailing to fellow prelates: 'It's not my head; it's my legs.'[10] He died the following December.

GEORGE VI – 12 MAY 1937

George VI's Coronation took place on the day that had been appointed for his brother's, Edward VIII's. The arrangements were well advanced. The main change was to include Queen Elizabeth in the proceedings.

There was more fumbling at George VI's coronation in 1937. Cosmo Gordon Lang, the splendidly thespian Archbishop, turned the crown this way and that, looking for a bit of red ribbon (which had been removed) and it was never clear if he put it on the King's head the right way round. At times Lang could be heard saying: 'Dukes, please stop talking … Ladies, please attend,' and 'Garter, where are you?' When the King rose and turned towards the throne, he later recorded: 'I was brought up all standing, owing to one of the Bishops treading on my robe. I had to tell him to get off it pretty sharply as I nearly fell down.'[11]

Osbert Sitwell thought the King looked like 'a medieval missal, grave, white & lean, & went through his duties with the simplicity of movement & gesture of a great actor.'[12] To this Cecil Beaton added: 'Since the King became so universally loved & his duties of kingship have been taken up with such great devotion, he has acquired an added beauty & nobility. It is the same metamorphosis that comes to a cinema star. As with his beauty, so his speech. The technical difficulties have been overcome & his voice is solemn, deep & emotional.' [13]

Queen Elizabeth [later the Queen Mother] arrived looking very grave, her little smooth brown head, unadorned, a contrast to all the tiaras – as she passed to her seat under the Royal Box, the Queen and all her ladies bowed to the Altar, and then came a gleam of a smile across her serious face as she saw the two eager little faces looking out at her from the Royal Box. During the service, Princess Margaret wriggled back into her chair and was much tempted to swing her legs, but Princess Elizabeth glared at her severely from the other side of the Princess Royal.

Queen Mary was so moved by the anointings that she was seen to cry. The Archbishop and the Earl Marshal edited that part out of the final film to be shown in cinemas. This show of emotion was used as an argument against televising the 1953 ceremony.

A Presbyterian divine shared his sandwiches with the Bishop of Durham, one of the King's supporting Bishops but when a Scottish peer offered him a draught from his flask, the Bishop 'thought it prudent to decline since the comfortable exhilaration might be too dearly purchased by the suggestive aroma.'[14]

As a Duke, the 10th Duke of Argyll had very much a front row seat at the proceedings. A high churchman he described the ceremony to a clergyman friend. We therefore have a ducal viewpoint and the Dukes he mentioned were described by their title alone:

> Richard Percy*, close by, very smart as Prince Arthur [of Connaught]'s Page was constantly swept aside when the Priests came in with the Regalia & all the Choirs of the Chapels Royal. We heard a fall down a wooden stair to our left & heard afterwards it was the Dean of Westminster & the Crown got all askew & was saved by its ribbons attached to the cushion!
>
> Cantuar did all the Coronation details admirably but the Mass was a poor show. He did not wear his mitre and as server did not even start the Chant of the Veni Creator. I really doubt if he even knows how to chant at all. Then he only bowed his head at the Incarnatus and did not kneel.
>
> At the homage - The murmur of the Earls was of course louder than ours. A whole gallery full of Barons above us whom I watched never knelt or murmured anything

---

* Lord Richard Percy (1921-89), son of the 8th Duke of Northumberland

it seemed to us. They seemed not to know the right moment & being many of them new peers probably did not know or recognise Mowbray & Stourton when he did his homage as the oldest of their order.

The Ceremony of the Recognition was so fine, done at the four corners of the theatre & the King in only his Cap of Maintenance looked like a real Fairy Prince. He did everything so solemnly and with unchanging expression. He bowed low so gracefully to us after our 4 shouts had been made.

To our immediate left had been propped all the morning the lovely golden canopy embroidered with silver angels, silver poles. Some hours earlier Atholl who is not very intelligent asked me what these 4 silver banners were! The 4 Garter Knights looked finer than anyone when they slowly stepped out, 4 heralds handing them the poles.

We could see the King in his white vest & breeks sitting ready for the anointing & then came his clothing in these special golden vestments, the close fitting Colobium Sindonis, the [Super]tunica, the Armill & a great cope like a cataract of gold, he slowly moved back towards us & ascended the theatre steps close to me and he was bodily lifted by elbows, feet and middle into his throne in the ancient way. All was so well done there was no ludicrous element about it. He kept himself no doubt passive and limp & then he is slight of build.

He & the Queen had certainly come fasting as they had much more colour after they had communicated & after the slight rest in their travoises by the Confessor's shrine. He really presented a most gorgeous spectacle, like some ancient hierophant & there can be no doubt that his mystic ring had wedded him to all his Realms for the masses of the Population have taken him to their hearts.

We only got a few sandwiches & biscuits 10/6 a head I had to pay £1 for a glass of sherry. No, it was not a guzzle by any means.

Then at 4, in buckets of rain we started to leave. Pandemonium there were no police. 12 miles of cars stretching to Lambeth & beyond the Tate Gallery. The awning dripped. One could not walk out & spoil ones robes. No one could get their car.

I waited 2½ hours. All sorts of Indian Princes & Ambassadors in the same quandary. I never saw my motor again nor did hundreds more. The last person only got away at 9pm!

Somerset had carried the Sceptre with the Cross so saw various things which we had missed. Furthermore he says the Dean of Westminster was like a half awake bat bewildered & incompetent, slow in all his actions. He kept laying out the Regalia in the wrong order on the mensa of the High Altar & each time put them differently. He twice gave the wrong sceptre and things to the various Lords. Some even said he did it to annoy Cantuar but I think it was just old age or illness (plus pomposity?)   Then when he gave Portland the Queen's Crown he got it hopelessly entangled in the Duke's Garter chain & it had to be unravelled & bits of the chain, Somerset thought, must have got bent!

I said to Marlborough 'I see you have come in gloves'. He said 'Yes. No pockets anywhere and my latch key is in one of them.' Then a shower of chocolates & meat lozenges fell out of his Coronet & he said 'I must see that does not happen when we put them on'. Atholl had filled his with the same objects & told me to warn him when he should empty it & he hid the uneaten residue under my chair.

Atholl said to me at the Enthronement 'And just to think how you & I were all about to take up our pens and refuse to attend Edward's crowning had he not abdicated.' For not 30 Peers would have attended out of the 700 or whatever it is.

Everyone says there were far too many ushers in the Abbey. When making for the P place to which I went only once, I asked one young frightened booby the way. He said 'You want to find your place?' I said 'You booby I have been sitting in it for 5 hours. I want the P. place.' He had no idea where it was! He was standing at the foot of the stairs down which the Dean had stumbled.

Malmesbury [Earl of] must have ruined his [robes] by his mad rushing about the street. They tell me he looked like a demented hen all huddled up. I wish I had seen the sight. He cannot keep quiet & is always in a fume and fuss.

Marlborough also drew my attention at 3 long intervals to Donegall* behind us

---

* 6th Marquess of Donegall (1903-75), a keen motor car enthusiast and journalist who wrote a column 'Almost in Confidence' for the *Sunday Despatch*.

to our right, who was sleeping profoundly. He is a scribbler in the newspapers. I said to M.: 'His description in the Papers will be all the more vivid of all that he had not seen!'[15]

As Princess Elizabeth, the Queen wrote an account of her father's Coronation. Today very few people now remember it. The Queen was one of the last survivors, but the Earl of Airlie (born 17 May 1926) was a page to his father. He and his wife were both present at the funeral and committal service for the Queen in September 2022.

Following the death of George VI, Sir Winston Churchill, Britain's great wartime leader, now back in Downing Street, but in somewhat indifferent health, saw the merits of a fine coronation. He wanted to put on a great show to boost the morale of a country still languishing under rationing and to eclipse the Festival of Britain of 1951, the great showcase of the previous (Labour) government. He would not do it in 1952 when the economy was weak and not a working day could be lost. For that and other reasons, a full year should pass. 'Can't have Coronations with bailiffs in the house,'[16] he declared. He wanted the coronation to herald a new age with a beautiful young Queen and her dashing husband as symbolic figureheads at the heart of the nation.

ACCESSION

A new sovereign succeeds to the throne on the death of his or her predecessor – 'The Queen is Dead. Long Live the King.' Automatic title to the crown was confirmed by the creation of a parliamentary entail in the 1701 Act of Settlement. Prior to this, the crown passed either by election, the hereditary right of one or other candidate often being disputed, sometimes in fierce battles prolonged into wars of succession.[17]

The two important constitutional acts were the Bill of Rights of 1689 and the Act of Settlement of 1701. These resulted from James II's flight from Britain in

December 1688. The King being absent from Britain, both Houses of Parliament deemed that he had abdicated, pronouncing on this with dramatic words:

> That King James the Second having endeavoured to *subvert the constitution* of the kingdom, by *breaking the original compact between king and people*, and by the advice of Jesuits and *other wicked persons* having violated *the fundamental laws*; and having withdrawn himself out of the kingdom, has abdicated the government, and that the throne is thereby vacant.[18]

James II had embraced Catholicism and Britain was determined never again to have a Catholic monarch. The Bill of Rights effected his formal Abdication in favour of William and Mary, both Protestants and grandchildren of Charles I. It required that the monarch swear a coronation oath to maintain the Protestant religion. This was still an integral part of the 1953 coronation and remains in the constitution today.

The Act of Settlement, passed in June 1701, went further by disbarring James II (still alive until September that year) should he try to reclaim the throne. It also excluded his Catholic son, James, the 'Old Pretender', and his daughter, Louisa (alive until 1712, though unmarried), and any of their descendants from inheriting the throne.

The Act selected the Electress Sophia of Hanover and her Protestant heirs and successors to inherit the crown. Sophia was a granddaughter of James I and a niece of Charles I. Thus the Act passed over numerous Catholic members of the Royal Family with a senior genealogical right. Though the crown remained in place, there were plenty of attempts to seize it, the Old Pretender – 'the King across the Water' – proclaiming himself King with the support of Louis XIV of France, the Jacobite Rebellion of 1715, and later the various exploits of his son, Charles Edward, known as the 'Young Pretender' or 'Bonnie Prince Charlie' but these were all in vain.

The Act of Settlement further stated that the monarch must be in communion with the Church of England. Because of this Act members of the Royal Family who marry Roman Catholics were until 2015 disbarred from the line of succession. It is still the case that the monarch cannot be a Roman Catholic.

So the crown passed by hereditary succession via Electress Sophia (who died just before Queen Anne in June 1714 – the Queen living until August) to four Hanoverian Georges in a row. The death in childbirth of the Prince Regent's daughter, Princess Charlotte caused panic in the Royal House as a result of which his brothers dropped their mistresses of long standing in favour of Protestant princesses of childbearing age. The Duke of Kent's wife produced the young Victoria, and after the death of George IV's next surviving brother, William IV in 1837, she succeeded as Queen Victoria and reigned for 63 years.

The crown passed smoothly from her to Edward VII, from him to George V and from George V to Edward VIII. There was a serious glitch in 1936 when Edward VIII abdicated in order to marry Mrs Simpson, passing the crown to his reluctant brother, the Duke of York. But it was only a glitch and the *Illustrated London News* merely chopped off King Edward's head and replaced it with King George's in the same image. The Instrument of Abdication was rushed through Parliament, and the departing King signed away his throne at Fort Belvedere, heading into a lifetime of exile. Princess Elizabeth succeeded her father as Queen on 6 February 1952. Because the new Queen was abroad when she succeeded to the throne, there were two Accession Councils. In the case of King Charles III there was only one.

THE STONE OF SCONE

In 1953 there was an issue over the Stone of Scone. It normally rested under King Edward's Chair in which monarchs sit when they are crowned. In earlier times the Stone lived at Scone Abbey near Perth, but had been captured by Edward I as a spoil of war and brought to Westminster Abbey in 1296. On Christmas Day 1950 the Stone was stolen by a group of Scottish students (one of whom Ian Hamilton went on to be a Scottish Nationalist MP and a QC), was smuggled into Scotland, repaired and finally left on the altar of Arbroath Abbey, from where it was rescued and taken back to Westminster.

The theft had been widely condemned, but the Scots were keen to have it back in what they deemed its rightful home. In May 1951 Lord Brabazon of Tara had tabled a motion in the House of Lords to the effect that the Stone should be returned to Scotland but brought down to London for each coronation. But Lord Simonds believed that as the Stone had been in Westminster Abbey for 600 years, there it should remain. The Dean had not yet had it placed back under King Edward's Chair, but with a coronation in the offing, Simonds was anxious to return it as soon as possible.

The Stone was replaced under the chair during evensong on 26 February. On the same day Churchill was quizzed on the matter in the House of Commons. He assured the House that all proper consultations had been made and then the Speaker intervened to say that any further questions must be held over to another day.

On 15 November 1996 the Stone was returned to Scotland. It was placed in Edinburgh Castle, to take its place in the Crown Room alongside the Honours of Scotland. In December 2020, following a public consultation, it was announced that the Stone would be relocated to Perth City Hall. This has not yet happened. The Stone of Scone will be returned temporarily to Westminster Abbey for King Charles's Coronation.

THE DECLARATION OF FAITH

The Declaration, as prescribed by Act of Parliament, is normally made in the presence of the two Houses of Parliament at a State Opening between the Accession and the Coronation. This is part of the process of being a constitutional monarch, the specific promise being to maintain the established Protestant succession. The Queen made her declaration at Westminster on 4 November 1952, on which occasion, not having been crowned, she wore the King George IV diadem. The Imperial State Crown was carried before her by the Marquess of Salisbury (Leader

'Didn't I tell you we'd rather die than
appear on television wearing our bifocals!'

of the House of Lords).

There was no State Opening between the Abdication in December 1936 and
the Coronation in May 1937, so George VI made the Declaration in the Abbey,
immediately after taking the oath. This oath changes each time. In 1937 George
VI was asked to swear to govern 'the peoples of Great Britain, Ireland, Canada,
New Zealand and the Union of South Africa' as well as his 'Empire of India.' The
Queen's oath was changed. She promised to govern 'the peoples of the United
Kingdom of Great Britain and Northern Ireland, Canada, Australia, New Zealand,
the Union of South Africa, Pakistan and Ceylon.' The new King's governance will
not include South Africa, Pakistan or Sri Lanka.

There is unlikely to be a State Opening of Parliament before King Charles III's
Coronation this May.

The words used by the late Queen were as follows:

I, Elizabeth II, do solemnly and sincerely in the presence of God profess, testify, and declare that I am a faithful Protestant, and that I will, according to the true intent of the enactments which secure the Protestant succession to the Throne of my Realm, uphold and maintain the said enactments to the best of my powers according to law.[19]

The Declaration will be made by the new King immediately after the Oath. The words are likely to be similar. Following that, the Coronation service can proceed.

THE CORONATION OF QUEEN ELIZABETH II

Preparation

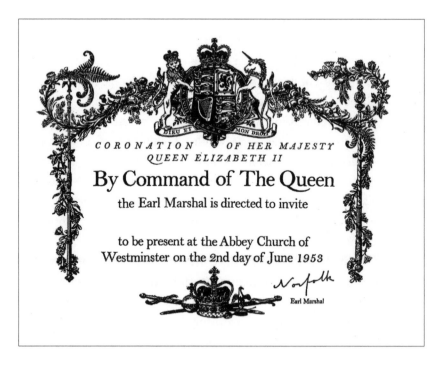

CORONATION OF HER MAJESTY
QUEEN ELIZABETH II

By Command of The Queen

the Earl Marshal is directed to invite

to be present at the Abbey Church of
Westminster on the 2nd day of June 1953

Norfolk

Earl Marshal

PREPARING FOR THE CORONATION

The Queen's Coronation ceremony was a long and complicated affair. It took many months to arrange. Liturgical matters had to be discussed and agreed, troops had to be mustered, the extensive programmes created and important figures had to be invited from overseas and in particular the Commonwealth. Every time new plans were announced, complaints poured in from politicians, journalists, members of the public and inevitably from Scottish Nationalists.

As soon as the date was announced, *The Times's* leader writer expressed the hope that 'with so long a time for preparation it is to be hoped that the ecclesiastical authorities will at last undertake the thorough revision of the rite itself for which liturgical scholars have been pleading at intervals for generations.'[1] Nor were Britain's mayors pleased. There was a change-over of mayors at the end of May each year. So the current mayor would do all the work while the incoming one took the credit as he presided over coronation celebrations.

A Coronation Commission was established to oversee the arrangements with senior British dignitaries such as the Archbishop of Canterbury and Cabinet ministers, along with senior Commonwealth Prime Ministers and High Commissioners. Conscious that he needed useful occupation, the Queen asked that the Duke of Edinburgh should chair the Commission with the Duke of Norfolk, the Earl Marshal, as Vice-Chairman. Prince Philip's appointment was announced at the end of April 1952.

As it turned out, the Duke only presided over two meetings of the Commission, one on 5 May and one when the Commonwealth Prime Ministers were meeting in London in December 1952, when they discussed the Coronation Joint Committee's recommendations on televising the ceremony. On both occasions the Committee members wore striped trousers and morning coats. He was also present with the Duke of Gloucester and others at a Coronation Committee of the Privy Council meeting on 16 February 1953 at which the form of the service and the music was discussed. The conclusion is that it did not interest him much.

This time people complained that the Moderator of the Church of Scotland and Lord Lyon King of Arms (senior herald in Scotland) had not been invited to sit on the Commission.

THE DUKE OF NORFOLK

All the arrangements (other than those concerned with liturgy) were left to the Duke of Norfolk.

Bernard, Duke of Norfolk, assumed his organisational role by hereditary right. All Dukes of Norfolk are Earl Marshals, and Duke Bernard had succeeded to the title at the age of eight and assumed his duties when he came of age in 1929. When still not quite 29 years old, he had arranged the coronation of George VI. He had been invalided out of the army after Dunkirk and given a wartime desk job. He was now a stout 45 years old, with the bearing of an older man. Most of his hair was artificially darkened and oiled down to his head. He suffered badly from gout, which he described to the broadcaster John Snagge as very 'discomfortable'.[2]

His duty was to summon the peers and peeresses, to send out all the invitations, to arrange the seating plans, decide on dress regulations, organise the processions and appoint the Gold Staff Officers. He surprised one divorced peer who feared that being divorced might mean he received no summons. 'Of course you will,' he said. 'This is a Coronation, not Royal Ascot.'[3]

No detail was too small to interest him. For example he made sure that the wood from which the platforms were made was properly seasoned. He did not want to hear the timber moving as the various figures climbed the steps.

The BBC commentator, Richard Dimbleby, was hugely admiring of him: 'Here was a man who carried the entire burden of the arrangements on his shoulders, who knew every detail, and personally worked on every timetable. I do not think that he could have had more than a few hours' rest at any time during the eight months preceding [the coronation].'[4]

In October 1952 the Duke set up an office at 14 Belgrave Square. His work frequently took him out of what would now be called his comfort zone. He appeared on television and he held press conferences. To all this he brought the full benefit of his inherited wisdom, combined with a dry, occasionally wry approach to whatever the media asked him. He was forced to point out that the Earl Marshal's Office was not one from which 'hot stories' would emerge on a regular basis. He made the important point that the Queen was taking a huge interest in the details of the ceremony and explained that this put an extra responsibility on him to make sure that all went smoothly on the day. He told the press that they deserved a good day and so did she.

At the major press conference announcing details of the ceremony, he expressed his appreciation of the way the press were handling their reports: 'I have read most of the articles and reports which have so far been published, and I am much impressed by the way in which, with very few exceptions, they combine accuracy, dignity and popular appeal – not always an easy combination to bring about'.[5]

A little later, the Duke borrowed his wife Lavinia to stand-in for the Queen at rehearsals. She was well versed in coronations, having been one of the Duchesses who had held the canopy over Queen Elizabeth when she was anointed in 1937. The Duchess appeared at the Abbey most days and, as we shall see, was even crowned by the Archbishop of Canterbury – albeit with a replica crown. She was a great asset at all the rehearsals.

THE COURT OF CLAIMS

The Lord Chancellor presided over the Court of Claims, which began as the Committee of Privileges, on which the Duke of Norfolk and others sat. Claims had to be made by petition by July 1952. As usual a number of peers and others petitioned the Court to be able to perform certain services by hereditary right. Twenty-one claims were made and in November sixteen of them were approved. For example the Dean and Chapter of Westminster were allowed to instruct the

Queen in the rites and ceremonies and to assist the Archbishop. They wanted to retain the robes and ornaments of the coronation and to have certain allowances and fees. The Court decided that the Queen could decide where the robes and ornaments were retained and she could also decide about the fees.

A prominent figure much heralded by Richard Dimbleby was the Honourable the Queen's Champion and Standard Bearer of England, Major John Dymoke, 33rd of Scrivelsby (1926-2015). He bore the Union Standard in the Abbey procession by ancient established rite and the Court of Claims were happy to confirm him for the role. He described his experiences in his diary:

> Never again shall I see such regalia and a wondrous collection of fine jewellery. The banks must have been empty on the day. We walked slowly down the aisle, thickly blue carpeted, to the strains of Handel and handed the Standards over to the Baron of the Cinque Ports and proceeded towards the altar. [6]

His claim dated back many centuries and was linked to the Manor of Scrivelsby. In 1377 his ancestor, Sir John Dymoke, fought and won a prolonged contest in the Court of Claims against another in the family, Sir Baldwin de Freville to be the Champion at the Coronation of Richard II. He based his claim on the rights of his wife, Margaret de Ludlow, 11th of Scrivelsby, granddaughter of Joan Marmion whose sister, Mazera, had married Ralph de Cornwall, and who was the maternal grandmother of the other claimant, Sir Baldwin de Freville. In those days the Champion would ride into Westminster Hall during the Coronation banquet, held there, clad in glittering armour of steel, a plumed helmet and mounted on a richly caparisoned horse. His specific role was to throw his gauntlet to the ground while a herald challenged anyone to declare their right to the crown, at which point the Champion engaged him in mortal combat. Invariably no such challenge was made, in which case the monarch drank wine from a gold cup in the Champion's honour.

Interestingly his grandfather, Francis S. Dymoke (1862-1946), who had been Champion at the Coronations of Edward VII, George V and George VI, became a recluse at Scrivelsby Court. When James Lees-Milne attempted to visit him on 21

August 1943, he was told that he had not been seen for years and the lodge keeper did not even know if Mrs Dymoke was alive (she had died on 25 May 1942). The lodge keeper delivered food to another man and it was put into a basket and pulled up to a first floor window. Lees-Milne clambered over a dry part of the moat and when he looked up he observed 'an ashen face with a snow-white beard, completely expressionless, pressed against the glass pane. As we continued round the outside of the house the same face appeared at every window, gazing down upon us vacuously.' [7]

Because they had done it before, the Bishop of Durham and the Bishop of Bath and Wells were permitted to be the Queen's Bishop Assistants throughout the ceremony, walking and standing either side of her.

Most claims were allowed, but not all. The Duke of Newcastle, as Lord of the Manor of Worksop, traditionally presented the glove to protect the Sovereign's hand while holding the sceptre. Unfortunately for him the Duke had recently placed the Manor of Worksop into a limited company – the London and Fort George Land Company Ltd – to oversee his estates. Accordingly this company claimed the right to present the glove but the Committee decided that they were not going to grant limited companies any rights over coronation regalia. The claim was rejected.

There was a thought that this part of the ceremony could be quietly dropped, but the Queen said she wished it retained. A few months later Lord Woolton was forced to resign as Lord President of the Council when he fell gravely ill with a perforated appendix and was close to death for a time. Though Woolton recovered, he realised he could never have held the Sword of State throughout the service. This role was undertaken by his successor as Lord President, the Marquess of Salisbury.

Lord Woolton was appointed Chancellor of the Duchy of Lancaster. He was excited when the Queen invited him to present the glove. The Duke of Norfolk told him: 'The Glove will be provided for you and all you will have to do is to go from the seat which will be allotted to you near-by at the appropriate moment (which will be indicated to you by a herald) and mount the steps of the Throne and present the Glove, assisting Her Majesty to put it on her right hand; and then retire.'[8] Woolton was advanced to be a Viscount in the Coronation Honours. He was assigned a seat behind Prince Philip so as to have the minimum distance to walk on the day.

The Court allowed the Countess of Erroll, premier Peer of Scotland, to be represented by a deputy, Lord Kilmarnock, as Lord High Constable of Scotland and for him to carry 'a silver baton or staff of 12 ounces weight tipped with gold at each end.' This provoked some anger that a lady was not allowed to take part herself.

The Court rejected the claim of the 17th Duke of Somerset to carry the orb or the Sceptre with the Cross, deeming that he had produced insufficient evidence of an hereditary right to do so. The Duke had petitioned to carry the orb at the coronation of George VI, on the grounds that his various ancestors and kinsmen had done so at all coronations since that of James II (other than the coronation of George IV in 1821 when the Duke of Devonshire carried it).[9] For some reason he was assigned the Sceptre with the Cross in May 1937. Rejected this time round, the Duke did not appear in the Abbey. He died less than a year later in April 1954.

Because there was no Coronation Banquet, the Court turned down Mrs Mary Long who wished, by virtue of her tenure of Heydon Hall, 'to carry the Queen's towel'. Nor would they allow Mr H.R. Boorman, owner of the Manor of Nether Bilsington, to present three maple cups, or to Rear-Admiral Edward Coker 'to act as the Queen's cup and standard bearer.' One claim went by default. A man calling himself 'His Highness Prince O'Brien of Thomond' based in Dublin had wanted to attend the coronation or 'to perform such other duty of privilege as may be decided.' His address was the Dalcassian Legation, Charlemont Street, Dublin.[10]

CORONATION ISSUES

The Prime Minister set up a small ministerial committee to give guidance on the scale of the coronation service. The Lord Privy Seal chaired this and the Home

Secretary and the Minister of Works comprised its members.

The Cabinet voted £1.5 million to pay for the coronation, this being broadly the same scale as for George VI in 1937, with an extra £0.5 million for army uniforms and service reviews. The Cabinet authorised the issue of No. 1 Blue Dress to all Army troops taking part at a cost of £205,000. They were not keen on service reviews, though when they later heard that a Naval Review could be held without additional expenditure, they agreed to it. (Presently, however, costs mounted on account of the need to entertain 1,250 distinguished guests and to hire three passenger liners for the purpose).

THE ROUTE

The processional route to the Abbey was to be the same as for George VI in 1937, a straightforward drive down the Mall, through Admiralty Arch and along Whitehall to Westminster. A key issue was the decoration of this route.

David Eccles was the Minister of Works and to him goes much of the credit for the visual impact of the coronation both in and out of the Abbey. He was an interesting figure, Sir Roy Strong recalling that he was known as 'Speckles' or 'Smarty Boots' and detecting an element of the second-hand car dealer about him. Eccles argued that the development of television and colour photography 'enhanced the importance of effective decoration on the processional route.'[11] The Cabinet allowed him £150,000 for decoration, floodlighting and fireworks. Eccles was responsible for the Mall being tarmacked red. He placed four arches, each 65 feet high, over the Mall, adorned with princess's coronets and a pair of wire lions and unicorns. Models of nine Queen's Beasts were placed outside the special annexe of Westminster Abbey.

Eccles stated that there had been 7,600 seats within Westminster Abbey in 1937 and that they could not squeeze one more in this time. This was not strictly true. In 1937 there were actually 7,606 and finally in 1953 8,064 seats were occupied. Outside stands would be provided for 98,000 people and it was stressed that these would not interefere with the traditional standing room which would be unreserved. Uncovered seats woud cost £3 10s, and covered ones (much needed on the day) would cost £5 10s. This was later increased to accommodate over 100,000 and Eccles said that a third of these would be allocated to Commonwealth and colonial visitors. Holders of the Victoria Cross, the George Cross, the Albert Medal in gold and the Edward Medal in silver were offered free seats.

Government buildings would be floodlit. He had consulted Constance Spry about floral displays and the royal parks were propagating thousands of flowers to be brought to perfection by the end of May 1953. Commonwealth flags would be much in evidence. These had proved popular at the Lying-in-State of the King.[12] He also requested £1,100 for additional lavatories in the Palace of Westminster.

Eccles had to balance his coronation duties and expenditure with overseeing housing programmes in areas being rebuilt after war damage. This required a delicate political balancing act.

Not only England celebrated with decorations and special exhibitions. By the end of May 1953 there were huge banners in the Boulevard Haussmann in Paris and store windows in New York were replete with models of the crown jewels and photographs of the Queen. Two thousand people an hour filed past a giant model of the coronation coach and horses at the Rockefeller Plaza.

PREPARATION OF THE SERVICE

Coronations follow a certain pattern but they are by no means identical. The service is not set in stone though it takes its primary source as the *Liber Regalis* dating from the reign of Edward II in 1308. The service has a threefold structure – (1) the promises taken by the monarch and the acclamation of the people, (2) consecration and anointing – the part of the Church, and (3) the vesting, crowning and enthronement, followed by the homage and then the receiving of the Sacrament.

Each coronation reflects the changing circumstances of the day. The Archbishop of Canterbury was determined that all should run smoothly, especially since it would be the most prominent event of his time in office. As the Dean of Westminster put it: 'The Archbishop of Canterbury … has it in his power to make or mar a Coronation.'[13]

The two men worked well together. Geoffrey Fisher was 66. He had been headmaster of Repton – 'a born disciplinarian, who achieved his ends by acting quickly, firmly and when necessary with severity,'[14] though posthumously he was to be maligned by Roald Dahl who confused him with a later headmaster and misidentified him as a sadistic caner of boys. Fisher was good at personal relationships, preferring the personal approach, and though not a courtier by nature, he got on well with the Royal Family, and had an 'almost fatherly concern for the young Queen.'[15] He had attended the coronation of George VI as a junior priest.

Alan Don, Dean of Westminster, 'a gothic-faced man in crimson cassock'[16] as he was described by one coronation guest, had taken a fuller part in 1937, serving as chaplain to Cosmo Gordon Lang when the Archbishop crowned George VI. A thin man, whose only contact with his wife was to lunch with her once a week, he had been associated with the Abbey for many years and had been Dean since 1946.

Neither Fisher nor Don were radical modernisers so that any calls for modernisation of the coronation found little favour with them. Certainly these calls came, most notably in *The Times* leader of 5 May 1952 which urged 'there can be no better occasion than this for divines, historians, and men of letters to combine to restore the Order to its proper perfection.'[17] The writer wanted the Oath revised, that Scotland be given better consideration and that Scottish peers and representatives of the Commonwealth do homage.

Later Clement Attlee made the reasonable suggestion that the Speaker of the House of Commons should do homage as a representative of the common man. Others suggested that the holders of real power such as the head of the Confederation of British Industry should take part. Sir Olaf Caroe, a senior civil servant, wanted the Governors General to take an active part, but there was a thought that if they did, then the Prime Ministers of India and South Africa would not attend. The Duke of Edinburgh also weighed in, asking the Archbishop if 'some features relevant to the world today could not be introduced.'[18]

One who intervened was a man destined to cause a huge furore in criticising the monarchy a few years later – Lord Altrincham (John Grigg after renouncing his peerage). He declared: 'Symbolism and ceremony are useless, and may even be harmful, if they do not express a reality.' He too was keen that the political changes be recognised. He was concerned that the Commonwealth would be under-represented. He offered to surrender his seat as a peer in favour of making the coronation a 'truly Commonwealth occasion':

Revival of the Enthronement in Westminster Hall, which was the ancient form till discontinued in 1831, might at first appear to conflict with the Commonwealth principle because it would concern members of the United Kingdom alone. But it would surely be splendidly justified if it made possible a reduced attendance of

United Kingdom peers and MPs in the Abbey, so that the representation of other Commonwealth Parliaments could be adequately provided for.[19]

None of this happened. Archbishop Fisher's biographer concluded: 'radical change would have proved difficult constitutionally and the Archbishop only half believed in the need to secure it. The Earl Marshal, who was ultimately in charge, did not wish it and the young Queen and her husband, though certainly in favour of modernisation, did not know how in practice to bring it about.'[20] The changes that were made never went further than aspects of detail.

The Archbishop began to contemplate the liturgical side of the service in July 1952. At that time he confessed to the Dean that he had 'so far had very little time to give to this serious matter'.[21] But by 1 August he had formed an advisory committee, comprising the Dean; L.G. Wickham Legg, who had attended the 1902 coronation and was the author of a book on coronation honours, living at Bodicote, in Oxfordshire surrounded by his father's coronation notes; Claude Jenkins, the Lambeth Palace librarian who had prepared the 1911 service; Professor E.C. Ratcliff, Ely Professor at Cambridge, a great expert on liturgy; and Professor Norman Sykes, one of Britain's most eminent ecclesiastical historians and later briefly Dean of Winchester.

From Professor Ratcliff the Archbishop received detailed notes. His precept was: 'The tradition of the English Coronation is not rigid and immutable like that of a Byzantine Imperial ceremony.'[22] Ratcliff traced the history of coronations back to the earliest days. The first time a Christian Anglo-Saxon King was elevated with a religious ceremony took place in 787, when Offa, King of the Mercians, designated his son Ecgfrith as his successor and he was anointed with oil.

The first recognised English coronation was that of King Edgar in Bath Abbey on Whitsunday, 973. There was a procession including nobles, clergy and nuns, and two bishops led the King into the Abbey by hand. The King prostrated himself before the altar while the *Te Deum* was sung and made a promise, the very earliest form of the coronation oath. The King was consecrated, anointed on the head while *Zadok the Priest* was sung. He was invested with the Ring, the Sword, the Crown, the Sceptre and the Rod. Each act of delivery was accompanied by a prayer, and the ceremony ended with a long benediction.

Coronation services developed over the centuries but became problematical with James II, a Roman Catholic who had no regard for a ceremony conducted by Anglican Bishops and who demanded that the communion service be omitted. Archbishop Sancroft altered the service considerably, causing 'not only abridgement, but mutilation, disturbance of arrangement and unnecessary alteration.'[23] When addressing the 1953 Coronation, Ratcliff noted that the 1937 service was substantially the same as that drawn up for the coronations of William III and Mary II as joint sovereigns in 1689. Further revisions had taken place between 1689 and 1838, and again at the coronation of 1902, and these had left their mark on the 1911 and 1937 coronations.

Ratcliff was keen to improve the 1953 service, noting that 'there is still scope for restoration and rearrangement; abbreviation and omission have reached a point beyond which they cannot go without detriment to the Rite, except in minor respects.'[24] Ratcliff was aware that preoccupations over the Abdication had left Archbishop Lang with too little time to make much needed revisions between December 1936 and May 1937.

Ratcliff wanted the holy oil blessed during the coronation service and not before; he thought it was meaningless to present spurs to a female sovereign; he wanted the orb omitted from the main service but for the Queen to carry it in the procession from the Abbey; he wanted to restore a prayer for the blessing of the crown; move the presentation of the Bible and many other such things.

The Archbishop wanted a meeting with Ratcliff in October and hoped to have the service in shape by December in order that the Queen could read it over Christmas.

One issue concerned the point at which the Duke of Edinburgh would do homage to the Queen – before or after the Archbishop of Canterbury. Of the four previous Queens Regnant (queens ruling in their own right), only Queen Anne had been married at the time of her coronation. Prince George of Denmark took precedence over the Archbishop. 'This may be held to constitute a precedent in relation to Princes of the Blood and the Peers of the Realm. In relation to the Archbishop and other Bishops, however, it was a breach in a long history.'[25] Prince Philip was not a man to care about such matters and he told Fisher as much when he came to lunch at the Palace in November 1952. So, on the day it was the Archbishop who did his fealty first. At that lunch, Prince Philip asked the Archbishop if he would be kissing the Queen on the cheek after doing his homage. Fisher replied that no, he wouldn't: 'I said that I regarded it as a very self-sacrificing act on my part, which tickled them both!'[26]

Ratcliff had maintained that only the Queen should 'communicate' but the Queen told the Archbishop firmly that she wanted Prince Philip included in the service. It was agreed that he would take communion beside the Queen and indeed a prayer was added for him in this part of the service. Pleased as he was to do this, the Archbishop made it clear in his notes: 'There must be no association of him in any way with the process & rite of Coronation.'[27]

Lawrence Tanner, Keeper of the Muniments at Westminster Abbey and author of a history of the Abbey, examined Professor Ratcliff's notes and, though he supported many of the suggestions, he occasionally found him 'not quite accurate' – as scholars have a habit of doing. He put up a strong case for the orb staying in the service as it was 'now so firmly fixed in the lay mind as an emblem of royalty that I venture to think that it would be a mistake – and indeed would arouse considerable comment – if it was no longer presented at the Service, nor do I like the idea of the Queen leaving the Church carrying an emblem of royalty which she has not received during the ceremony.'[28] Curiously he did not seem to mind the Queen wearing the Imperial State Crown, which did not appear until the Queen emerged from St Edward's Chapel after the Recess at the end of the service, to process from the Abbey.

When the Archbishop announced the coronation service plans, he said that in 1689 the then Archbishop had not realised that the orb duplicated the sceptre which contained an orb of its own. He said that iconoclasts would have got rid of the orb but 'I am all in favour of anomalies; therefore we have kept the Orb and given it more prominence than it had before.'[29] He did not say that he longed to smuggle the Rod with the Dove into St Edward's Chapel after the service and hand it to the Queen, replacing the Sceptre with the Cross, to save her from carrying two orbs.

There were discussions as to how to refer to the various swords, what to do about 'Amens' and the wording of the coronation oath to reflect changes in the Commonwealth. The oath was referred to the Prime Minister and he obtained approval from all the Commonwealth countries so that it reflected the new constitutional position created by the Indian Independence Act and various other statutes.

The Archbishop chose that the Moderator of the General Assembly of the Church of Scotland would present the Bible to the Queen immediately after she took the Oath recognising Scotland's part in the United Kingdom. The handing over of the Bible then and not at the time of crowning provoked a strong howl of protest from the Bishop of Rochester.[30]

Sometimes the exchanges between the Archbishop and the Dean were humorous. The Archbishop wondered if it was correct to say the Queen would be 'lifted up' into her throne. The Dean responded: 'It is a quaint phrase which rather appeals to me, and though some confusion would doubtless ensue if the Archbishops and Bishops attempted to carry out the rubric literally, I am disposed to think that it is not worth while making any alteration.'[31] The phrase 'lifted up' stayed in.

By March 1953 the Queen had read and approved all the changes and the Archbishop of Canterbury was ready to announce them at a press conference at Church House, Westminster. In the weeks before the ceremony, the Archbishop devised special readings for the Queen to help her understand the different aspects of the coronation. He also preached sermons on consecration, majesty and dedication in order to prepare the general public for the service. One of the points he made was:

The Queen has not chosen this office for herself. She comes to it because it is laid upon her. She is called to it by God: and she accepts it at his hands.[32]

THE MUSIC

Music is a fabulous feature of all coronations. Originally the Chapels Royal influenced most of the music. Then for the coronation of George II, Handel composed four great anthems – *The King shall rejoice, Zadok the Priest, Let thy hand be strengthened* and *My heart is inditing. Zadok the Priest* (or 'Zodiak' as the Duchess of Norfolk called it to the amusement of the Archbishop) has been sung at every subsequent coronation. George IV so loved Handel that he entered the Abbey to the *Hallelujah Chorus*. Later Elgar made memorable contributions and in 1902 Sir Hubert Parry wrote *I was glad*, now a permanent feature. So while some music became an expected part of the great ceremony, there was still always room for new musical challenges.

The Archbishop consigned the musical programme to Dr William McKie, the Abbey's Organist and Master of the Choristers. He immediately consulted Sir Adrian Boult and Sir William Walton, and formed a committee consisting of Sir Ernest Bullock (who had been organist at the Abbey for the 1937 Coronation), Sir William Harris (organist of St George's Chapel), Dr Stanley Roper of the Chapels Royal and Dr John Dykes Bower from St Paul's Cathedral.

They commissioned eight new works, amongst which was a hymn that all the congregation could join in at the offertory, an idea much supported by the Queen and the Archbishop – Ralph Vaughan Williams's rearrangement of *All People that on earth do dwell*, complete with fanfares. New works came from Herbert Howells and Healey Willan (from Toronto) and there was a concluding *Te Deum* from Walton – on a tremendous scale for choir and orchestra, with organ and trumpeters. Walton also composed the now famous *Orb and Sceptre* march.

In 1902 there had been some 430 singers with musicians massed in stands behind the High Altar. In 1937 and in 1953, to the annoyance of British women, some Commonwealth ladies were invited to join the choir, which by then was augmented to 400 men and boys with an orchestra of 60. McKie made a note not to have women another time.

McKie spoke of how he dealt with the choir: 'Our work in training boys is uncommonly like training performing animals. Good choirboys have most of the pleasanter qualities of the nicest dogs. They are lively, cheerful, trusting and faithful. They are sagacious and have excellent memories'.[33]

In 1953 the music was judged to be a triumph though the Archbishop, not a man entirely attuned to musical appreciation, wondered afterwards if there had not been too much of it.

THE QUESTION OF TELEVISION

One of the most controversial issues that loomed in Cabinet discussions was the question of television. The Queen and her advisers were originally against television coverage. In a memorandum of 7 July 1952, John Colville briefed the Prime Minister, arguing that 'live television would not only add considerably to the strain on The Queen (who does not herself want television) but would mean that any mistakes, unintentional incidents or undignified behaviour by the spectators would be seen by millions of people without any possibility of cutting or censorship'.

Colville was aware that this was likely to be an unpopular decision. He felt it important that the Cabinet should endorse a decision supported by the Earl Marshal, the Archbishop of Canterbury and the Dean of Westminster, along with the Coronation Joint Committee.[34] It was endorsed.

The Cabinet said that the departure from Westminster Abbey could be filmed, but no part of the service. In 1937 there had been a cinema film after which the Archbishop and the Earl Marshal edited out scenes such as Queen Mary in tears at the anointing. For 1953 they thought that an edited film showing the service could be slotted into TV coverage to be shown later in the day. In so doing they hoped to avoid unnecessary strain on the Queen and respect the sanctity of the occasion.[35]

One who objected strongly to the decision not to allow TV inside the Abbey was the Venerable Francis House, Head of Religious Broadcasting at the BBC, who lived until 2004, dying aged 96. He was a fascinating man who, in his early life, had undertaken numerous dangerous journeys through Europe rescuing Jews from Nazi Germany. He was aware of the decline in church going, but saw how hymn singing and church services relayed via the wireless and television could reach people in their own homes. To him goes much of the credit for eventually reversing the decision.

House was convinced that it needed to be filmed and told the Dean of Westminster that the Bishops of London, Bristol, Liverpool and St David's, all of whom sat on the BBC Central Religious Advisory Committee, had no objections. His argument was:

> Why should millions of Her Majesty's loyal subjects be deprived of the possibility of joining in full in the Coronation Service and be put off with the processions (without religious significance) outside and inside the Abbey, and with the short film of extracts of the Service which would be shown in the cinemas?[36]

He pointed out that the Queen would not have additional stress since she was already being filmed, that it could all be done on 'long shot' without close-ups, and that TV lighting was less strong than that needed for films. Francis House was much supported by George Barnes, Director of Television at Broadcasting House. The Archbishop worried about close-ups, noting that the Queen had a habit of licking her lips, but the Dean began to be won over and approached the Earl Marshal.

As late as 4 August 1952 the Duke of Norfolk was holding firm. He pointed out that the Coronation Commission, the Coronation Privy Council Committee and the Cabinet were unanimously against television. He declared that 'religious services should not be made the means of providing Television Programmes', and he rammed home the final point – that he could edit things out, but 'Live Television goes straight to the World and any mistakes can never be rectified, and to my mind this is very important.' [37] While the Duke was against it, Sir George Bellew, Garter King of Arms, was all for it.

A public announcement was made on 20 October saying that television coverage would be restricted to the processions west of the choir screen, with an edited film of the ceremony shown later. There was an instant uproar of criticism in the press. Even the *Church of England Newspaper* commented: 'Nobody conducts these occasions with such dignity as the authorities of the Abbey and of the Court. Then why not let everybody see it who can? The Monarchy in this country is not an underground movement.' [38] Sir Alexander Cadogan, Chairman of the BBC, did not like the decision and was prepared to intervene but he thought it more effective to let the thwarted viewers protest. They did so in droves.

MPs asked questions in Parliament. Within the Cabinet, Lord Salisbury was against it, while at first Churchill stated that it was not a Government decision. 80 Labour MPs tabled a motion deploring the Prime Minister's refusal to disclose details of the advice given by the government. In a guarded statement Churchill agreed to re-open discussions.

Behind the scenes Lord Swinton and David Eccles were pro-television. The Cabinet Secretary, Sir Norman Brook, admitted that television was here to stay and thought the Cabinet should move with the times. But he warned, perhaps with prescience: 'May this not be an awkward precedent? If the Coronation ceremony is televised, what argument will remain for refusing television facilities of e.g. Royal funerals or weddings, religious services and even proceedings in the House of Commons?' [39]

In those days there was a rule that no camera could come closer than 30 feet to the Queen. Peter Dimmock, Television Outside Broadcast Producer and Director of the Coronation for the BBC, was able to show the deciding powers how it would look, seen through the cameras. Fortunately, in those days, Archbishops, Deans and Dukes of Norfolk were not technical experts. Dimmock was careful to employ a wide angle two inch lens for this demonstration. They were reassured that it would not be intrusive.

Churchill told the Cabinet that it was hard to defend a decision to discriminate between film and television. But he still believed that 'the spiritual parts of the proceedings' should be excluded from both, in particular the anointing and the prayer of consecration. His idea was that 'no more intimate view would be given than that which would be available to the average person seated within the Screen'. There should be no close-ups of the Queen.[40]

The Archbishop was especially worried about the prayer of consecration and warned Francis House: 'It is all right for people in quiet homes and hospitals and so forth, but we have to remember that it will also be broadcast on the stands, all the way that the procession is afterwards going, and one cannot guarrantee there any question of stillness.'[41]

Lighting was another problem. The lights were hot and the Archbishop was concerned as he was bald. No Archbishop had worn his mitre during the ceremony since the coronation of Elizabeth I, but Dr Fisher wore his when processing in and out. One Bishop said nothing would induce him to wear a mitre but they could not do so since they needed chaplains. So bald tonsures went unprotected.

The final decision about television rested with the Queen and her advisers. Whereas there is no doubt that she had not been keen on the idea at first, she is credited with having the foresight to change her mind and see the benefits. Certainly when Cabinet papers were released in 1983 exposing her initial reaction, figures such as Sir John Colville and Sir Edward Ford were quick to point out that she saved the day. Colville claimed that the Queen had told Churchill that 'all her subjects should have an opportunity of seeing it.'[42] On 8 December the Earl Marshal announced that most of the coronation would be televised.

CELEBRATIONS

The Queen was keen that celebrations should be widespread but let it be known that she wanted them to be simple and not incur unnecessary expenditure. During the summer months of 1952 announcements were made in respect of special stamp issues throughout the Commonwealth, the planting of trees, the creation of souvenirs and of special exhibitions to be held.

The London County Council announced there would be fireworks and displays of aquatics on the South Bank, that the illuminations would outshine those for the Festival of Britain, that 30,000 children would be enabled to see as much of the processions as possible, and that 400,000 children would be presented with special propelling pencils. Holders of medals were told they could wear them on the day and relatives of deceased holders could wear the medals on the right-hand side.

Welcome news came to publicans. The Metropolitan Police extended the licensing laws from normal evening opening times until midnight for those pubs within half a mile of the coronation route on 1 June. Pubs could open all day on coronation day and those with specific functions until 3 am. Midnight opening was extended from 3 to 6 June. The Minister of Food allowed a bonus of 1 lb of sugar to be added to the ration (still in place in 1953). Ox-roasting was permitted 'provided that it was undertaken by responsible bodies only'.[43]

In October 1952 the Queen's rather shy aunt, the Princess Royal, made an appeal that Britain should tidy itself up before the coronation to give a good impression to foreigners. Speaking in Harrogate, she particularly deplored houses and shops 'plastered with advertisements like pages from an untidy scrapbook', not to mention general untidiness and litter.[44]

AMNESTIES

The question of granting amnesties to deserters from the Second World War on the occasion of the coronation came before the Cabinet. The arguments were that 'it was not in the national interest that these men should continue to live the lives of outcasts and outlaws.' But service ministers maintained that 'an amnesty for deserters would be taken as implying that desertion in war was no longer regarded as the most serious of military crimes, and would lead to increased desertion from the armed forces at a time when very large numbers of men were serving overseas in circumstances which imposed the most disagreeable duties upon them'.[45] On 24 March 1953 the amnesty was granted, allowing deserters to apply for a protection certificate.

ACCOMMODATION

The London Hotels Information Service announced that they would co-ordinate bookings in the capital to make it easier for visitors, following similar arrangements for the 1937 coronation and the Festival of Britain, when they had fielded 250,000 enquiries. The Dorchester built an eight storey addition above their banqueting rooms, to provide thirty more bedrooms, Oliver Messel designing a special suite, while the Savoy Hotel promised not to increase the cost of rooms during the coronation season. Londoners were also asked to rent rooms to foreigners where possible. Renters were discouraged from over-charging and by and large they observed that.

There was no shortage of overseas visitors wishing to be in London in June 1953. Another way of housing them was to moor six passenger ships in the the Thames to providing beds for 3,400 visitors. To get them into contemplative mood, there was a special programme to place 50,000 bibles in London hotel rooms, boosted by a gift of $100,000 from the Gideons to kick start the scheme.

PUBLIC REACTION

All these plans added to the mounting excitement of the coronation, but seaside resorts began to worry where they would find the normal military bands to entertain their visitors in the summer of 1953.

In a more general sense it took some time for the British public to get excited. This is quite usual with impending celebrations and certainly happened again at the time of the Silver and Golden Jubilees.

The coronation was being staged in a country suffering the effects of wartime expenditure and damage. Rationing was still in place. The economy was not in a good state and many were suffering hardship. As always there were some who were thrilled by every aspect of the unfolding plans, who watched London being transformed for the great spectacle with ever-growing excitement, but there was also a small minority who wished to take no part in it – the cynics, a few republicans, some earnest modernisers.

CHRISTMAS MESSAGE

On Christmas Day the Queen made her first Christmas message from Sandringham, sitting in the same chair that her father had always used. She thanked the people for their loyalty and affection since her accession ten months before. She asked for their support at the coronation:

> At my Coronation next June I shall dedicate myself anew to your service. I shall do so in the presence of a great congregation, drawn from every part of the Commonwealth and Empire, while millions outside Westminster Abbey will hear the promises and the prayers being offered up within its walls, and see much of the ancient ceremony in which kings and queens before me have taken part through century upon century.

> You will be keeping it as a holiday: but I want to ask you all, whatever your religion may be, to pray for me on that day – to pray that God may give me wisdom and strength to carry out the solemn promises I shall be making, and that I may faithfully serve him, and you, all the days of my life.[46]

1953 dawned and Westminster Abbey closed its doors to prepare for its transformation.

PREPARATION OF THE ABBEY

Preparation of the Abbey for the service took several months and so the Abbey was closed for services from 1 January 1953. In his last sermon before the closure, the Dean of Westminster said that for any other reason than the Coronation this would be 'a grievous deprivation' but 'by this time next year it would be seen that it had been worth while.'[47]

Such was the enormity of the works that a railway line was installed up the central aisle to convey the building materials to the specially constructed theatre east of the choir stalls. The Royal box was built on the south side of the Abbey and bore the arms of the Queen and the Duke of Edinburgh. Tier upon tier of boxes were constructed, most of them facing inwards so that as many guests as possible could be invited and afforded good views of the processions. The sides of the galleries were hung with a blue silk warp tissue patterned in gold with repeated motifs of national emblems beneath crowns.

Unlike at coronations in previous centuries, there were no seats allowed above and behind the altar. Though this meant less invited guests, one reason was that this made it a spectacle more than a service. As the present Dean of Westminster has pointed out, King Edward's Chair faces the altar, emphasising that the Sovereign makes his or her pact with God, unlike in Hollywood films such as *The Prisoner of Zenda* where the King faces the congregation (or would they be called guests?). The royal dukes had throne-like chairs, each adorned with his coat-of-arms. Behind them the peers sat on coronation chairs, covered in blue velvet and bearing the cypher 'E II R'. The other guests sat on some 5,701 specially made stools.

Five Glasgow girls, working five abreast on one of the widest looms in the world, were amongst a large team busily weaving thirty-one gold and blue carpets for the Abbey. The carpets were made from chenille Axminster with very short pile so as not to impede the passage of the robes and trains of peers and peeresses. The central theatre, sanctuary and side aisles of the Abbey required twelve carpets, the

One of the specially made chairs.

largest being 86 feet by 32 feet. The cost was estimated at £18,500.

Many of those present in the Abbey, especially those in the Nave, would not be able to see the ceremony itself. They would only see the processions in and out and hear the voices and the music. But nevertheless it was a great honour to be present.

In order to marshal the many complicated processions, a magnificent annexe was built outside the Great West Door and long tables placed there on which the Regalia could be placed. It was designed by Eric Bedford of the Ministry of Works. By 11 April 1953 it was very much in evidence, as were the spectator stands opposite the Abbey. The annexe contained retiring rooms and robing rooms for the benefit of those who had ridden in the procession. This kind of annexe had been a feature of all coronations since that of William IV, designed to match contemporary styles.

INVITATIONS

As with any major event, the question of who to invite and who to exclude proved a complicated one. The Abbey would eventually seat just over 8,000 people. A great many more than that wished to come.

Peers of the Realm traditionally played a major part in coronations. For 1953 there were problems about the considerable number of them who wished to attend. Knights of the Garter and Thistle, holders of the Order of Merit, Companions of Honour or those who held Grand Crosses were safe. So too were the three surviving Knights of St Patrick, though they were all too old to be there. Widows of peers could only apply if they were Dames Grand Cross of British Orders or held the Order of the Crown of India.

Applications for a summons had to be in by 1 December 1952. At the end of the month the Earl Marshal announced that there were not enough seats and suggested that peers could apply for two free seats in an outdoor stand and buy an extra two. A ballot would be needed for those to be summoned to the Abbey.

Peers were not pleased. Lord Derwent pointed out that if enough peers reserved outside seats no ballot would be required. Lord Devonport suggested that those peers who took part in House of Lords committee work should have precedence over those who did not attend regularly. Lord Glanusk objected 'most strongly' to Lord Devonport's hint that 'we who seldom enter the House are slackers and neglecting our privileges and duties.'[48] He pointed out that he needed an income to support his family and so could not attend as often as he would wish.

Not all peers were summoned. Bankrupt peers in particular caused headaches in parliamentary circles and at the College of Arms. One issue was whether or not being bankrupt prevented a peer from attending. In 1937 Sir Claud Schuster, Permanent Secretary at the Lord Chancellor's Office, had examined the precedents. He found that in 1911 an Irish peer, the Earl of Clancarty, had been summoned and did attend, despite having been adjudicated bankrupt in September 1910. But he could not find an absolute ruling. He thought common sense and what was 'convenient and proper' should be the yardsticks: 'I do not see how any peer to whom, for whatever reason, a summons has not been issued could by any legal process insist upon a right to receive it.'

He thought that the matter of invitations 'should be determined by the Pleasure of His Majesty,' adding wryly, 'the true question is in what way His Majesty should be advised to exercise that Pleasure.' In the end Schuster pronounced himself dead against summoning bankrupt peers, or notorious, albeit unconvicted peers and certainly not peers who had 'fled the Realm in order to avoid criminal proceedings, whether for a felony or a misdemeanour.' Nor would their wives be summoned.[49]

The senior peer in each category traditionally does homage to the monarch on behalf of the other peers of his rank. Thus, after the Dukes of Edinburgh, Gloucester and Kent, it was the Duke of Norfolk.

The privilege of doing homage for the Marquesses was granted to the Marquess of Huntly, because the premier Marquess, the Marquess of Winchester, was excluded from the service being a bankrupt. This did not prevent his Indian wife commissioning a portrait of herself by Frank O. Salisbury, showing her adorned in a golden sari and the Coronation robes she was not allowed to wear. It hangs outside the Bapsy Room in the Town Hall, Winchester. There was more trouble in store for Monty Winchester. He had been nearly 90 when he married Bapsy. Rather unsportingly she sued him for non-consummation of the marriage.

The eccentric 5th Lord Rayleigh, a descendant of the scientist who discovered argon, did not receive a summons. But as he had lately stood up in church on his 7,000-acre Essex estate and declared: 'I am the King of England', there was cause for concern. Fearing that he might disrupt the coronation, his family had him spirited away to the West of Ireland and made sure that he just missed every possible train that might reach a boat from Dublin so that there was no chance of him getting to the church on time.[50]

In April 1953 the Earl Marshal sent summonses to the chosen peers with the words 'Right Trusty and Well-Beloved Cousins' urging them not to fail to attend. They were given admission tickets, car parking instructions and details of lunching plans.[51]

The Duke of Windsor was amused that the Marquess of Bath wanted to arrive at the Abbey in his coach while the Metropolitan Police was equally determined that he would not. The Duke recalled that in 1902 'more than one noble Lord made history – and drew upon himself the dirty looks of his fellow peers – by arriving at the Abbey in a spluttering motor car.'[52]

* * * * *

At the same time, specific commands were issued concerning robes, coronets, the collars of Orders to be worn. Peers were to wear full dress uniform under their robes, the problem being that none had been issued since 1938. They were permitted to wear any robes that had been used at previous coronations. The Duchess of Devonshire (Deborah Mitford) therefore cut a fine figure in the unusual robes of Duchess Georgiana, which she found in a tin trunk at Chatsworth. Lady Diana Cooper had her late mother's ducal robes adapted to those of a Viscountess.

The Earl of Harewood was irritated that he could not wear his father's coronet as an Earl. He had to wear the coronet designated for grandsons of the sovereign, which had to be ordered specially at a certain expense. 2,000 swords were ordered from the Wilkinson Sword Company in Acton for those taking part.

The couturier, Norman Hartnell, was commissioned to design a new style of robe for Viscountesses and Baronesses whose families did not already possess them, though it was his assistant, Ian Thomas, who drew the new designs. They disposed of the traditional kirtle and long train, creating one garment which subtly united the two, minimising both. They produced a neat red velvet cap to be worn behind the tiara. Surprisingly perhaps, these designs found favour with the traditionally-minded Earl Marshal and when submitted to the Queen, they were approved.

The rest of the congregation were also given dress instructions – mantles and collars for Knights Grand Cross, civilians to wear evening dress with knee breeches, but morning dress or dark lounge suit was permitted (the latter worn by Aneurin Bevin to the ill-concealed irritation of the diarist and MP, 'Chips' Channon). Ladies without robes could wear tiaras or veils on the backs of their heads. No hats or coats could be worn but a light wrap could be worn. There was a further note: 'Oriental dress may be worn by ladies and gentlemen for whom it is the usual ceremonial costume.'[53]

The Queen gave the Dean and Canons some striking blue copes with a lion and unicorn on the back. 'We're the Dean's beasts', joked one of them.[54]

* * * * *

The Royal Family were allowed to invite a number of guests, the number according to their status. These were named in the Lord Chamberlain's List.

Members of the extended Royal Family sat in the Royal Gallery, ranging from the Queen Mother to Sir Henry and Lady May Abel Smith, the Marquess of Milford Haven, and Lady Mary Whitley and her husband. A seat was kept for the young Duke of Cornwall (Prince Charles). Prince Philip's sisters were there with their husbands - Princess Margarita of Hohenlohe-Langenberg, Margravine Theodora of Baden, and Princess George of Hanover. None of them had been invited to the wedding of the Queen and Prince Philip in 1947. This time the sisters were determined to be there. As early as March 1952 they 'fixed that in Philip's mind!!'[55] They were duly invited with their mother, Princess Andrew of Greece, who led them out of the Abbey and was singled out by Cecil Beaton as 'a wonderful contrast to the grandeur, in the ash-grey draperies of a nun.' [56] Her brother, Earl Mountbatten of Burma, was prominent on the day, weighed down with orders and decorations. As Edith Pye, his mother's elderly maid, put it: 'Prince Dickie was simply magnificent. Absolutely a Coronation in himself!' [57]

Members of the Royal Family were allowed to invite certain guests. In the days of Edward VII, this meant that the box in which he placed his various mistresses was nicknamed 'the Loose Box'. In 1953 the Royal Family sat in the Royal Gallery. Besides the British Royal Family and Prince Philip's immediate relations, there was Princess Astrid of Norway (who descended from Edward VII through her grandmother, Queen Maud of Norway), and also in the box were Sir Horace Evans (the Queen's physician), Miss Helen Lightbody (Prince Charles's nanny) and Nigel Loring (Apothecary to the Royal Household).

In The Queen's Box were Bowes-Lyon relations, Elphinstone and Granville cousins – all relations on her mother's side, and some interesting figures such as the Count and Countess of Barcelona (he being pretender to the Spanish throne), Norman Hartnell (who had designed the Queen's Coronation dress), 'Bobo' Macdonald and her sister, Sir John Weir (the homeopathic doctor whose treatment of the late King had been so questionable) and other personal friends, such as Lord Euston (later Duke of Grafton) Lord Porchester (later Earl of Carnarvon), the trainers, Noel Murless and Sir Cecil Boyd-Rochfort, and some of her Household, Jock Colville and his wife Lady Margaret, and Lady Mary Strachey (an early lady in waiting).

The Queen's Seats cast the net a little wider – Prince and Princess Frederick of Prussia, the Mayors of Windsor and of King's Lynn, the portrait painter James Gunn and others.

The Duke of Edinburgh's guests were largely his German relations, the young Badens, Hesses and Hohenlohe-Langenbergs. His page's parents were included and the most unusual guest in the Abbey was Baroness de Buxhoeveden, who had been lady-in-waiting to his grandmother, the Dowager Marchioness of Milford Haven, and previously to her sister, the Tsarina Alix of Russia (who was murdered in 1918). In 1937 she had been invited by Princess Louise, Duchess of Argyll (daughter of Queen Victoria).

The Queen Mother invited family and Household and old friends such as the aesthetic writer, Sir Osbert Sitwell. Queen Mary had also invited some guests, mainly Household, but Terence Cuneo amongst them. Though she had died before the Coronation, they were there on the day. Princess Margaret had friends, the Gloucesters had her relations, and the Princess Royal had mainly Household.

Princess Marina, Duchess of Kent had nephews and nieces, Yugoslavs and

Toerrings. Princess Elizabeth of Yugoslavia wore a much remembered dress from Dior in Paris, and when Princess Marina's nephew, Count Hans Veit Toerring applied for permission to be away from school for some days in Germany, the reason stated in the book was 'Coronation of a relative.' [58]

It was traditional that no other crowned heads ever attended coronations. Queen Louise of Sweden was furious that as the wife of a King, she could not be there since she was Prince Philip's aunt. Since they were also close relations, King Paul and Queen Frederika of Greece wanted to attend the service and challenged the custom but were instead represented by the King's uncle, Prince George of Greece, dressed in the robes of the Order of the Bath, accompanied by his wife, the former Princess Marie Bonaparte, a distinguished lay psychoanalyst who briefly reverted to royal status for the occasion.

Emperor Haile Selassie of Ethiopia was represented by the Crown Prince, and the Kings of Iraq, Laos, Nepal, Norway and Saudi Arabia were represented by their Crown Princes, other Kings by other members of their families – the King of Afghanistan by his uncle (Marshal Shah Wali Khan), Queen Juliana of the Netherlands by her husband, Prince Bernhard, the King of Thailand by Prince Chula (who lived in Cornwall), and so forth. These three and the Crown Prince of Norway were the only ones to have also attended the 1937 coronation. Prince Chula's wife, Lisba, loved the occasion, feeling 'as if she was in an old painting she had seen in some gallery,' as her husband put it. [59]

Since diplomatic relations had been resumed with Japan in 1952, some years after the Second World War, it was appropriate that Emperor Hirohito should send his 19-year-old son, Crown Prince Akihito, as his representative. As soon as this plan became known, the Foreign Office considered the situation. John Pilcher observed that the Ambassador, Sir Esla Dening had 'hinted at the gaucherie of the Crown Prince and the possible necessity of his receiving a little coaching in western ways before coming over here for the Coronation.' [60] The problem was that the Crown Prince showed no disposition to talk, even in his own language.

When the Crown Prince came to dinner at the British Embassy, he told the

Ambassador he hoped to attend the Derby and Ascot while in the UK, and was anxious not to miss Wimbledon. 'These are healthy signs,' wrote the Ambassador, 'and it is to be hoped that his wishes can be gratified'.[61] Half a million Japanese gathered to give him a rousing send off on his sea journey at the end of March. He arrived in Britain on 27 April. In due course the Queen did invite him to the Derby and on the day of the coronation he took his place in the choir stalls. He was given a coronation medal and remembered to wear it when, as Emperor, he paid his 1998 state visit to Britain.

The Archbishop of Canterbury also played a part in reconciling Britain and Japan. In 1948 the Bishop of Kobe had attended the Lambeth Conference. He presented the Archbishop with a wonderful cope, specially worked by churchwomen in Japan. The Bishop told the Primate that this was a peace offering, following the terrible things that had happened in Japan during the war. The Archbishop chose to wear this cope for the coronation, a gesture which caused no adverse comment, possibly because the media were then less pro-active in stirring up public feeling.

Royal guests who were heads of their countries could be invited as long as they came from British colonies. These were Queen Salote of Tonga (of the Friendly Islands in the Pacific, who proved such a success with the crowds by sitting in an open carriage in the rain), the Sultan of Zanzibar (in the Indian Ocean), the Sultans of Johore, Selangor, Kelantan (soaked opposite Queen Salote) and Perak (all parts of the Federation of Malaya), the Sultan of Brunei (a British Protectorate on the North West coast of Borneo), and the Sultan of Lahej (part of the Aden Protectorate). So too were invited the Kabaka of Buganda (King Freddie, who died mysteriously in London in 1969) and his wife, the Nabagereka (part of the Uganda Protectorate); and Mwanawina, Paramount Chief of Barotseland (part of Zambia).

The Commonwealth was most particularly represented: countries such as Canada, Australia, New Zealand, South Africa, India, Pakistan, Ceylon and Southern Rhodesia sending dozens of important figures over, including, usually their Prime Ministers. In July 1952 the Cabinet was told that Shri Jawaharlal

Nehru, Prime Minister of India, would accept an invitation if the Queen offered him one. She offered and he accepted but in January 1953 he told Lord Swinton, the Colonial Secretary, that nothing should be done involving him, 'which anybody in his country could criticise.'[62]

Early in the new reign, Dr Borg Olivier, the Maltese Prime Minister, declared that Malta would not be represented at the service and that he had cancelled plans for coronation festivities on the island. Churchill was determined that he should come, Malta being the George Cross island. Concessions were made. The Blue ensign with the Arms of Malta was dropped in London in favour of the red and white flag and Churchill gave him a place in the procession of Commonwealth Prime Ministers. Meanwhile the Cabinet had some difficulty in persuading the various Commonwealth Prime Ministers to share coaches, of which there were a limited number. Malta joined the Commonwealth in 1964.

The Archbishop of Canterbury supplied the names of Bishops and in certain cases, their wives. The Scottish Office dealt with representatives of the Established Church of Scotland, who were not allowed their wives. The Archbishop consulted Cardinal Griffin of the Roman Catholic Church about his possible attendance. The Cardinal did not feel he could be there, but, in response to the Queen's request for prayers, he directed that the three days prior to the coronation should be a 'triduum of prayer that God may bless her Majesty and her realms' and he asked that 'the entire Catholic community in England and Wales be united in prayer for the Sovereign on the eve of the Coronation itself.'[63]

The Lord Chamberlain's Office, the Foreign Office and the Privy Council Office provided names and the Speaker of the House of Commons submitted the names of MPs and their wives (many of whom took the option of outdoor stands with excellent views of the procession). And many other offices provided other names as appropriate.

Then there were those who were not invited. The Duke of Windsor was neither a bankrupt nor a felon but he was not summoned. The Queen raised the question with the Archbishop of Canterbury when he lunched at Buckingham Palace in

November 1952. It was agreed that 'it would create a very difficult situation for everybody, and if he had not the wits to see that for himself, then he ought to be told it.'

Similarly Winston Churchill decided that although it was understandable that the Duke would wish to be present at family funerals, it was completely inappropriate that he should be present at the coronation of one of his successors. It seemed it would have to be the Queen who told him.

Once the Archbishop saw which way the land lay, he took the precaution of going to see Sir Alan Lascelles, the Queen's Private Secretary. Lascelles's view was that 'a hint to the Duke that he was not wanted might only incite him to want to come.' Lascelles took the precaution of writing to the Duke's lawyers, Allen and Overy, making it clear that no invitation would be coming.[64]

It was agreed that the Duke would tell anyone who asked that it was inappropriate constitutionally for a previous monarch to attend such a ceremony.[65] Nevertheless, when interviewed at Cherbourg, the Duke must have alarmed the British Government by suggesting that 'very probably' he would be in London at the time of the coronation.[66] In the event the Duke and Duchess stayed in Paris, the Duke consoling himself by writing some well-paid articles, later published as a little book – *The Crown and The People* 1902-1953.

Another man excluded was Sidi Mohammed ben Yusef, Mohammed V, Sultan of Morocco, who was determined to be there. By October 1952 he was becoming anxious, fearful that the French might intercept his invitation. He was keen that the British Consul-General in Fez should deliver the invitation personally and, in anticipation of it, announced that he was having some valuable jewels mounted by his private craftsmen in the Mellah Fez to present to the Queen. These were mainly emeralds dating back to the reign of Moulay Ismail, Warrior King of Morocco from 1672 to 1727.

The Foreign Office pondered this issue. They were keen to be courteous to the Sultan, but they did not want to upset the French. Morocco had been a French Protectorate since 1912 and the Sultan's sovereignty was subject to him not entering into direct diplomatic relations with foreign states. Therefore he did not come into the category of those Heads of State to whom an invitation would be sent.

There was a kind of precedent in relation to Emperor Haile Selassie of Ethiopia and King Victor Emmanuel III of Italy at the 1937 coronation. Both intended to send their Crown Princes. 'A rather undignified argument arose and finally Haile Selassie was asked to withdraw his son and only appoint one representative', it was noted, but it was also accepted that this was not a direct precedent that provided useful guidance.[67]

It was clear that the Sultan himself could not attend 'his Sovereign status, no less than French objections, would forbid it. Equally he cannot send Prince Moulay Hassan, or anybody else, as his representative.' There was an idea that the Queen might invite him as a personal guest, but it was feared that this might upset the French. It was left that the British Embassy in Paris would consult the Quai d'Orsay. Meanwhile, there remained the problem of the jewels: 'In any event, we must try to head off those emeralds. The Queen has ruled that as a general principle She does not wish any gifts to be made to Her on the occasion of the Coronation.'[68] The Sultan stayed at home.

Another who was 'most perturbed' at not being invited to attend or send a representative was the last Bey of Tunis (later King of Tunisia until he was deposed in 1957). He was already in trouble with the French Government and no doubt thought the coronation would be a welcome diversion. The Foreign Office did not care about him, the question of his invitation was never raised officially and he did not come either.[69]

THE GREAT OFFICERS OF STATE

On 14 January 1953 the Earl Marshal announced a number of special appointments, including those Great Officers of State who were not already in place.

The Lord High Steward was appointed just for the day. His post was established before the reign of Edward the Confessor and he was originally the principal officer under the Sovereign. The role used to be hereditary but was then merged with the crown in the fourteenth century. Since 1421 the position has been vacant and only granted to a subject for a few hours at a time, and then only at at coronations (or the trials of peers and then generally occupied by the Lord Chancellor). By long established tradition, the Lord High Steward carries St Edward's Crown at the coronation.

The man chosen was Admiral of the Fleet 1st Viscount Cunningham of Hyndhope, KT, GCB, OM, DSO (1883-1963). He was one of the great leaders of the Second World War, serving as Commander-in-Chief, Mediterranean Fleet. His victories included the attack on Taranto in 1940, and the Battle of Cape Matapan (in which the Duke of Edinburgh served) in 1941. Admiral Cunningham defended Mediterranean supply lines through Alexandria, Gibraltar and Malta and directed naval support for the major Allied Landings in the Western Mediterranean littoral. He was First Sea Lord from 1943 to 1946. On the day of the coronation he wore his robes as a Knight of the Thistle.

When he died in a London taxi on 12 June 1963 (just ten years after the coronation) on the short journey between Parliament Square and Waterloo Station, a friend said: 'It was typical of his modesty and of his never bothering people about himself that he just got into a taxi and went straight to heaven.'[70]

The second Great Officer is the Lord High Chancellor – Lord Simonds, a Cabinet Minister already involved with numerous issues concerning the Family name, the Stone of Scone and the Declaration of Faith.

The third Great Officer is the Lord High Treasurer. From 1126 until 1612, this was held by one man. Subsequently there have been Lord Commissioners of the Treasury, so no one individual was Lord High Treasurer in 1953.

The fourth man, the Lord President of the Council, was the 5th Marquess of Salisbury, KG, PC (1893-1972), who held the Sword of State throughout the ceremony.

Lord Salisbury was an influential Conservative minister, who served as Lord

President from 1952 to 1957, having taken over following the enforced retirement of Lord Woolton through ill health. He was acting Secretary of State for Foreign Affairs (June to October 1953). Later in the 1950s, he was a key figure in the selection process for a new Conservative Prime Minister. 'Which is to be?' he asked back benchers. 'Wab or Hawold?' He descended from Robert Cecil, 1st Earl of Salisbury (himself the son of William Cecil, Lord Burghley, the celebrated Treasurer of Elizabeth I). He was a personal friend of the late King George VI, and had been appointed a Knight of the Garter in 1946. At one Garter ceremony Lord Montgomery looked disparagingly at Salisbury's robes and ventured that they looked rather tired. 'Mine have had to serve several generations,' came the laconic reply, 'whereas yours were made new for you.'[71] Lord Salisbury carried the Imperial State Crown at the State Opening of Parliament in November 1952. He carried out his duties at the coronation with difficulty due to a weak back. When he knelt, he had to be helped to his feet.

The fifth Great Officer is the Lord Privy Seal (or sometimes more formally Lord Keeper of the Privy Seal). In 1953 the post was held by Rt Hon Harry Crookshank (1893-1961). He had served in the Grenadier Guards in the First World War and been severely wounded. In a subtle euphemism, his friend, Oliver Lyttelton, wrote: 'His grievous wounds prevented him from living a full private life.'[72] He had been castrated by a shell splinter in 1916. He rose through the Foreign Office to Parliament, becoming a Cabinet Minister belatedly. As Lord Privy Seal he led the House of Commons. On the day of the coronation, 'Chips' Channon spotted him amongst the Great Officers of State who 'swished their robes with dignity. Harry Crookshank without, of course, a coronet amongst them.'[73]

The Lord Great Chamberlain is the sixth of the Great Officers. He has charge of the Palace of Westminster and plays an important role at the coronation, with the right to dress the Sovereign on the day. The role being hereditary, the peer who occupies it still maintains a seat in the House of Lords in 2013 in order to fulfil his ceremonial role, despite most of the hereditary peers being excluded.

The Lord Great Chamberlain was the 5th Marquess of Cholmondeley, GCVO

(1883-1968). His office passes in a complicated way from one family to another, changing with each new reign. It is hereditary and the same family has it for each reign. The Queen was served by three Marquesses of Cholmondeley in succession. The new Lord Great Chamberlain is the 7th Lord Carrington.

In other reigns it goes to other families. For example, it was the Marquess of Cholmondeley in the reigns of William IV, Edward VII, Edward VIII and that of the present Queen, whereas Queen Victoria was served by the 22nd Lord Willoughby de Eresby and then 1st Earl of Ancaster; George V by the 1st Marquess of Lincolnshire and then Viscount Lewisham (as Deputy); and George VI by the 2nd and 3rd Earls of Ancaster. It must have been galling for Lord Cholmondeley to have the short reign of Edward VIII, though he was compensated by 16 years of service to Queen Elizabeth II.

Lord Cholmondeley was described by Lord Salisbury as 'an aristocrat in the best sense of that much abused word.' The former actress, Maxine Elliott described him as 'probably Apollo.'[74] He perfected the most beautiful calligraphic script. He was married to the immensely rich Sybil Sassoon, whose family were banking sheiks in Baghdad. They lived at Houghton in Norfolk, the former home of his ancestor, Sir Robert Walpole, close to Sandringham. At the 1937 Coronation he had carried the Royal Standard.

Lord Cholmondeley had a most active role at the coronation and was much in evidence directing operations and assisting the Queen with costume changes, with much needed help from the Mistress of the Robes, since he was not adept with buttons. He carried a white wand of office. Anne Glenconner, a maid of honour as Lady Anne Coke, described him:

> The Marquess of Cholmondeley was the most handsome man and he seemed very proud of his looks – he always sat bolt upright with his head slightly to one side. The trouble was, he was simply terrible at doing up hooks and eyes, probably never having had to dress himself, let alone anybody else. [75]

The Duke of Norfolk arranged that the hooks and eyes were changed to poppers, but when the Marquess pressed the poppers, he pushed the Queen 'rather violently', which as she told Anne Glenconner later was 'tiresome'. [76]

The seventh of the Great Officers of State is the Lord High Constable. In earlier times the Lord High Constable was Commander of the Armies and Master of the Horse. He was President of the Court of Chivalry and martial law was undertaken in his name. His powers are so considerable that since 1547 the appointment is only granted for the day of the coronation and then immediately cancelled. The 1st Duke of Wellington served in 1821, 1831 and 1838, the 1st Duke of Fife (son-in-law of Edward VII) in 1902 and 1911, and the 1st Marquess of Crewe in 1937.

Field Marshal Viscount Alanbrooke, KG, GCB, OM, GCVO, DSO was the man chosen for the job. He had been Chief of the Imperial General Staff during World War II and Churchill's closest military adviser, the two men frequently at loggerheads but ultimately appreciative of each other's virtues. Alanbrooke was therefore one of the most important strategists of the Second World War. On the day he rode in the coronation procession and inside the Abbey he wore the robes of the Order of the Garter.

The eighth Great Officer is the Earl Marshal. We have already seen the Duke of Norfolk at work. And the ninth is the Lord High Admiral, a position held by the Queen throughout her reign until, in June 2011, she gave it to the Duke of Edinburgh on his 90th birthday. So there was no Lord High Admiral on duty as such at the coronation.

Another appointment was that of Great Steward of Scotland, as Deputy to the Duke of Rothesay (the 4 year old Prince Charles). He was the 28th Earl of Crawford and Balcarres, KT (1900-75), a well-known custodian of the arts in Scotland.

Other key figures in the ceremony were the Lord Chamberlain and the Mistress of the Robes. The 11th Earl of Scarbrough had taken over the role of Lord Chamberlain from the Earl of Clarendon, who had been lame since his Eton days when he fell down stairs and broke his hip, answering a fagmaster's boy call. He was advised that the long ceremony would be too strenuous. His successor had served as a most successful Governor of Bombay and during his time in India it had fallen to him to arrest Gandhi and other political leaders in 1943.

The Mistress of the Robes was also newly appointed. Mary, Duchess of Devonshire, was a sister of the Marquess of Salisbury, thus uniting the great houses of Cecil and Cavendish. She had been widowed in 1950 when her husband had a heart attack whilst chopping wood, causing prolonged negotiations over death duties with the Commissioners of the Inland Revenue. She processed immediately behind the Queen and assisted her with her various changes of robe. For the anointing she was grateful that Norman Hartnell designed the white linen overdress with large buttons and buttonholes so that she could manipulate them while herself wearing white kid gloves.

Six Maids of Honour were appointed to carry the Queen's train and to help remove it and fold it before the anointing. They were:

Lady Rosemary Spencer-Churchill (born 1929), daughter of the 10th Duke of Marlborough.

Lady Jane Vane-Tempest-Stewart (born 1932), daughter of the 7th Marquess of Londonderry.

Lady Mary Baillie-Hamilton (1934-2022), daughter of the 12th Earl of Haddington

Lady Anne Coke (born 1932), daughter of the 5th Earl of Leicester

Lady Moyra Hamilton (1930-2020), daughter of the 4th Duke of Abercorn

Lady Jane Heathcote-Drummond-Willoughby (born 1930), daughter of the 3rd Earl of Ancaster

* * * * *

On 14 January 1953 the Earl Marshal also announced others who had been appointed to walk in the Grand Procession.

There were six standards to be carried. The first was the Union Standard to be borne by Captain J.L.M. Dymoke, by virtue of holding the manor of Scrivelsby and thus to be the King's Champion apparently since 1377 (though this date was contested). The Standard for the Principality of Wales was carried by Lord Harlech, KG, and then came the Standards with the quarterings of the Royal Arms, Ireland held by Lord De L'Isle and Dudley, VC, Scotland by Viscount Dudhope, and

63

England by the Earl of Derby. The Royal Standard was carried by Field Marshal Viscount Montgomery of Alamein, KG, wearing the robes of the Garter.

As had been traditional at most coronations since that of Henry VI in 1429, four Knights of the Garter were chosen to hold the canopy over the Queen during the Anointing. They were more or less the four most junior, presumably since these were likely to be the fittest – Viscount Allendale, Earl Fortescue and the Dukes of Wellington and Portland. These Knights had all been friends of the late King, which indicated 'a preference for personal friends which, if persisted in, would do the Order no good.'[77] Cecil Beaton was amused to spot the Duke of Wellington there:

> It was all very dignified but I had a moment of private amusement to see Gerry Wellington so serious as he held the lances of the canopy. I would like to have seen his face if I had shouted to him that Sidi Azaid had a message for him, for during the war in Cairo Gerry used to behave very badly in an Arab bath which was subsequently closed down.[78]

At the same rehearsal James Lees-Milne observed the peers wearing coronets that looked like 'washstand basins with feet sticking up' and commented: 'I saw Gerry Wellington under his, worn at a scornful tilt like an old dowager's toque.'[79]

THE REGALIA

Then there was the Regalia, which would rest on a large altar-like table in the Annexe. Most of the Regalia dated from the coronation of Charles II in 1661, since earlier regalia had been melted down during the phase of the Commonwealth. The new pieces were commissioned by Sir Edward Walker from Robert Vyner, a Goldsmith. It was said at the time that it cost £13,000, a sum equivalent to building three ships of the line. An exception was the spoon that accompanied the ampulla, used by the Archbishop for the anointing. The spoon survived from the twelfth century and had probably been made for the coronation of Henry II. It is divided down the middle, enabling the Archbishop to sweep his fingers along two separate parts. All the Regalia resided and still resides in the Tower of London. In theory the Regalia were brought from the Tower just before the coronation on 1 June, but in reality from the offices of the Goldsmiths and Silversmiths where they had gone for cleaning and restoration.

On the day the Marquess of Cholmondeley handed the Regalia to the peers chosen, in the following order:

St Edward's Staff – 3rd Earl of Ancaster.

The Sceptre with the Cross – Marshal of the RAF 1st Viscount Portal of Hungerford.

The Golden Spurs – 21st Baron Hastings & 4th Baron Churston.

The Pointed Sword of Justice to the Temporality (or Third Sword) – 8th Duke of Buccleuch & Queensberry.

The Pointed Sword of Justice to the Spirituality (or Second Sword) – 14th Earl of Home.

Curtana, Sword of Mercy – 10th Duke of Northumberland.

The Rod with the Dove – 9th Duke of Richmond & Gordon.

The Orb – Field Marshal 1st Earl Alexander of Tunis.

The Sword of State – The 5th Marquess of Salisbury.

St Edward's Crown – Admiral of the Fleet 1st Viscount Cunningham of Hyndhope.

The Paten – Rt Hon & Rt Rev William Wand, 112th Bishop of London.

The Chalice – Rt Rev Alwyn Williams, 92nd Bishop of Winchester.

The Bible – Rt Rev Percy Herbert, 67th Bishop of Norwich.

The Regalia Peers were largely establishment dukes and famous war leaders. Amongst them was a future Prime Minister, Lord Home, better known to us as Sir Alec Douglas-Home. They all did a good job, but, perhaps inevitably the one who was destined to cause the most trouble was one of the least well-known, Lord Hastings, who would prove vociferous and demanding at the rehearsals (*for more details on the Regalia Peers see the Appendix*).

* * * * *

The Queen at Buckingham Palace, April 1953.

Princess Elizabeth on the balcony of Buckingham Palace after the Coronation of George VI, 1937, with the King and Queen, Queen Mary and Princess Margaret.

Models in the salon of Norman Hartnell – an alternative Baroness, a Baron and a Marchioness.

Outside the Abbey before a rehearsal
– the Duke of Wellington with his
page and grandson, Jeremy Clyde –
the Duke of Portland behind in the
hat.

The Duke of Norfolk greeting the Queen
before a rehearsal.

Gentlemen at Arms going through their
paces.

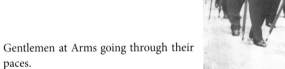

The Archbishop of Canterbury.   The Dean of Westminster.

Princess Margaret processing in. Behind her, from left to right, Mr Malik (the Soviet Ambassador), Prince and Princess Himalaya of Nepal, Crown Prince Akihito of Japan, & Crown Prince Abdul Illah of Iraq. Indira Gandhi, later Prime Minister of India, is third from the left in the second row. Queen Salote of Tonga is visible in the back row.

The Earl Marshal (the Duke of Norfolk) with his pages, Hon James Drummond and Duncan Davidson.

The Anointing – the Canopy Knights – Earl Fortescue to the left, Viscount Allendale to the right.

The moment of crowning.

The Queen crowned in King Edward's Chair, with her Assistant Bishops – Durham (left) and Bath and Wells (right).

The Queen enthroned. Behind her Lord Simonds (the Lord Chancellor), and Viscount Portal of Hungerford.

The Duke of Edinburgh does homage. On the right is Lord Hastings who presented a spur.

Sir Winston Churchill follows the Prime Ministers of Canada (Louis St Laurent) and Australia (Robert Menzies) out of the Abbey. Waiting to the right, the Officers of Arms (including front right – Dermot Morrah, and back left, Anthony Wagner, with Lord Lyon King of Arms in the centre), then the Duke of Edinburgh and his suite. Behind more Officers of Arms, then the Regalia Peers. Top left: The Earl of Home.

The Queen and the Duke of Edinburgh on the balcony of Buckingham Palace. Prince Richard of Gloucester to the right.

The Queen processes out of the Abbey.

The Queen about to enter the Gold State Coach.

When the various appointments as to who was carrying what were announced, the special correspondent to *The Times*, again probably Dermot Morrah (though not named), wrote: 'The most notable feature of the announcement is that no attention has been paid to the plea that the Commonwealth should be given an active share in the Coronation by appointing some of the Queen's oversea subjects to hold some of theose ceremonial offices which are at the Sovereign's disposal, or to carry parts of the regalia.'[80]

Emanuel Shinwell, the Labour MP who would live to be 101, declared that in the democratic times in which they now lived, there should have been 'great and illustrious scientists, those from the medical profession, nurses, miners, farm workers, steel workers and railwaymen. These are the salt of the earth ... I hope that those in authority will give a thought to the changes that have occurred in the last 50 years and realize that the aristocracy is doomed and almost damned.'[81] The only Commonwealth link was the gift of the Armills or Bracelets traditionally presented to the Sovereign. The traditional Armills dated from 1661 but Robert Menzies, Prime Minister of Australia, suggested that new ones should be made and this idea was taken up by the United Kingdom government and the government of Southern Rhodesia and were eventually the gift of all the Commonwealth countries. They were specially made by the Crown Jewellers.

THE QUEEN'S DRESS

Credit must go to the Queen's aunt, the Duchess of Gloucester, for the eventual choice of Norman Hartnell to design the magnificent dress she wore at the coronation. In 1935 Lady Alice Scott, as she then was, commissioned him to design her pearl-pink wedding dress when she married Prince Henry. Princess Elizabeth and Princess Margaret were her bridesmaids and so he designed dresses for them too. At the fittings he caught the eye of their mother, Queen Elizabeth.

At the 1937 coronation Queen Elizabeth felt she must remain loyal to Madame

Handley-Seymour, who had designed her wedding dress in 1923. The resulting dress was correspondingly undistinguished. But the Queen Mother chose Hartnell to design the dresses for her Maids of Honour and afterwards transferred her patronage to him and the well-known crinolines followed.

Hartnell went on to design Princess Elizabeth's wedding dress in 1947 and a number of other outfits for her, notably for the 1951 tour of Canada. As we have seen, he was also commissioned to design some new versions of robes for certain peeresses at this coronation.

In October 1952 Hartnell was delighted to be invited by the Queen to design her dress. She wanted it to be similar in line to her wedding dress. Hartnell studied the precedents and then retired to his house at Windsor Forest and produced eight different designs veering from the simple to the elaborate. The eighth sketch contained the heraldic emblems of Great Britain, including the Tudor rose, the thistle and the shamrock and a daffodil (which Hartnell then believed to be the national emblem of Wales).

This inspired the Queen to ask for emblems of the Dominions of which she was also Queen and led to a ninth and final design. Meanwhile Hartnell ran up against Garter King of Arms who objected strongly to the daffodil, telling him firmly: 'No, Hartnell. You must have the Leek.'[82] Hartnell retreated home and pulled up a leek from his vegetable garden. He was suitably disheartened by its appearance. Luckily he then remembered that the leek was the emblem of the Welsh Guards and 'in the end, by using lovely silks and sprinkling it with a dew of diamonds, we were able to transform the earthy Leek into a vision of Cinderella charm.'[83]

Hartnell then worked on the other emblems – the maple leaf of Canada, the wattle flower of Australia, the fern of New Zealand, the protea of South Africa, the lotus flower of India, wheat, cotton and jute for Pakistan, and a different lotus flower for Ceylon.

A visit to Sandringham and an improvised fashion show produced the necessary approval. The Queen Mother and Princess Margaret ordered their dresses and Hartnell also designed dresses for the Maids of Honour, concentrating particularly on the back of the dresses because, as they were carrying the trains, this was likely to be seen as prominently as the front if not more so. The Maids of Honour wore the headdresses that had been worn by the Queen's bridesmaids in 1947.

He went on to design dresses for the Duchess of Kent (Princess Marina) and Princess Alexandra, not to mention a great many peeresses. Nine girls worked on the Queen's dress, three on the dress, and six on the embroidery. At first they were not told that this was indeed the dress. Throughout the process, there was intense security, the girls working in a secluded room, the only access through the office of Hartnell's ever-vigilant private secretary, Mrs Price.

The royal purple velvet for the Queen's train was commissioned from Warner and Sons in Braintree, Essex, the raw silk from Zoë, Lady Hart Dyke's silk farm at Lullingstone, to then be thrown at the Glemsford Silk Mill in Suffolk. More than twenty yards were hand-woven at the rate of a yard a day. When it was ready it was sent to the Royal School of Needlework to be embroidered and turned into the traditional royal robe. It was emphasised that every ingredient of the robe would be British, including miniver from the best Canadian ermine. Work began in November 1952.

On 12 May 1953 Hartnell was ordered by his doctors to take a rest. He was in a run down state due to overwork. But he was back in action at the end of the month when the Queen summoned him to the Palace. The coronation dress (concealed in a large cardboard box) was delivered to the Palace in the Hartnell van and smuggled in through a side door. Hartnell himself followed in a taxi to 'keep an eye on it.'[84]

When the Queen saw the finished dress, her comment was 'Glorious.'[85] Hartnell's première fitter, Isabelle Fowler, always known as Madame Isabelle, watched the Queen's face reflected in a mirror: 'Never have I seen such happiness.'[86] And in the Abbey itself, Hartnell spared a special thought for 'the Duchess of Gloucester and all that I owe to her.'[87]

QUEEN MARY

Queen Mary's health failed gradually following the death of her son, George VI, though she was able to take a great interest in the forthcoming coronation of her granddaughter. As we have seen, in June 1952, she took the Queen to the Museum of London, then at Kensington Palace, to show her the necessary robes of state. In the early weeks of 1953 she used to be driven out from Marlborough House to see the coronation stands being erected. She knew she was not strong enough to be present in the Abbey and therefore loaned her 1937 train to the Queen Mother.

One announcement caused Queen Mary particular grief. A stickler for precedence, she was shocked to learn that the Duke of Edinburgh was going to ride to the coronation in the Gold State Coach sitting beside the Queen. She thought he ought to ride on horseback like the Duke of Gloucester as a Personal ADC.[88]

In the same month Queen Mary went into terminal decline and died at Marlborough House on 24 March. It was stated that she had left instructions that should she die in the period before the coronation, she did not want it to be postponed.

By this time it was too late for the Queen Mother to move into Marlborough House. Clarence House was nearly ready for her and in May 1953 she moved there from Buckingham Palace, taking Princess Margaret with her, a not wholly comfortable arrangement. When MPs complained about the cost of refurbishing Clarence House, the Queen Mother wrote: 'Perhaps they would like me to retire decently to Kew and run a needlework guild?'[89]

Queen Mary's death left a great void. As the Queen said to her Private Secretary, Sir Alan Lascelles, it was hard to think of a world without her.

BROADCASTING PLANS

Covering the coronation on radio and television was a considerable operation and took months of planning. There would be four cameras in the Abbey, one above the high altar, one by the south transept, one in the organ loft and one at the west end. There were 26 microphone points, most of them near the Queen's throne.

John Snagge expected the job of commentating for the BBC Home Service to go to a clergyman as it had done in 1937. Snagge was best known as the 'Voice of the Boat Race', their commentator from 1931 (and continuing until 1980). So he was surprised to be chosen. He discussed where the microphones should go and found that the Duke of Norfolk remembered exactly where they had all been in 1937. This time they were concealed in many subtle ways.

Snagge was worried about what he would do if the Queen fainted under the heavy robes and hot lights or if a peer carrying the Regalia should fall over. He was to operate from a minute, unventillated box in the triforium, in the company of Howard Marshall. He guided them through the service and Marshall described the scene. Snagge wrote: 'It was very cramped indeed; we were packed in like a couple of sardines.'[90] On the day itself it was estimated that 83% of the population listened to his commentary.

Above him, in slightly more comfort, was the ample figure of Richard Dimbleby. He was to commentate for television. Dimbleby lived on a yacht in the Thames during the run-up to the big day. He attended numerous rehearsals and knew the ins and outs of every part of the service by the time the day arrived. He owed his spectacular view of the proceedings to the Duke of Norfolk, who climbed up to the triforium one day to choose the best vantage position.

Below Dimbleby, Snagge and Marshall were the television cameraman, again in cramped surroundings. And there were overseas commentators. The sound proofing was so effective that any of them could have shouted at the tops of their voices and no one in the Abbey would have heard them. Audrey Russell was in the annexe for a sound commentary as was a Continental counterpart.[91]

The Postmaster-General asked that television coverage should be extended more widely over Britain as there were still areas that were not covered. For this new stations had to be built. 21 mobile television units and other units meant that the BBC's five high-power transmitters would relay the ceremony to 83%

of the country's population, but even so it was impossible to extend coverage to Southampton, Plymouth or Aberdeen in time for June.

 Plans were made so that the ceremony could be seen on television in France (a small but well-publicised effect being that the Duke and Duchess of Windsor were able to watch it), Western Germany, the Netherlands, Belgium and other European countries. BBC recordings were to be flown to Canada in Canberra bombers and on to the United States so that it could be seen within hours of the event.

A number of televisions were installed in churches in Britain so that the congregation could watch and 'surround the Queen with their prayers' as one rector put it.[92] On the day the Home Service started broadcasting on the wireless at 5.30 am, featuring numerous interviews with Commonwealth Prime Ministers before covering the procession and service, the Light Programme largely provided music, while the Third Programme kicked off with Kirsten Flagstad singing songs by Greig and repeated a sermon used at the coronation of William and Mary. Television tuned in at 9.15 am and was live on the coronation until 5.20 pm.

Television sets were widely purchased by private individuals – 27 million people settled down to watch. To this day survivors remember their first experience of television as watching the flickering black and white images moving about small screens in their own homes on that memorable day.

* * * * *

Looking at the television coverage in retrospect it is interesting to note the position of the cameras. There was a camera above the Great West Door so that as the procession entered the Nave for the ceremony, you only saw them from behind. Such a thing would not be tolerated today. Admittedly they were seen in full splendour as they entered the choir. This enabled a good view of the procession on the way out – but not on the way in. There was another camera above the High Altar and there were cameras in that part of the Abbey so that the ceremony was well seen from several angles.

It helped that the entire commentary was conducted by Richard Dimbleby on whom fell the burden of identifying each distinguished figure as they arrived. Being well rehearsed, he did a good job. It is fair to say that the commentators were beginning to get into their stride by 1953. In the earlier commentaries, it sometimes seemed that these former war correspondents found ceremonial less stimulating than their war experiences. But as peacetime settled on the land, they appreciated that the viewers wished to be informed. Even so it was hard for him to have every detail to hand. It is a shame that this precision appears to have been dropped by present day commentators.

THE REHEARSALS

The coronation was rehearsed in every possible detail. The first troop rehearsal took place on a cold and frosty morning in November 1952, taking one hour and 35 minutes to complete the five mile route.

As early as 5 am on two Sunday mornings running in May, a crowd of several hundred gathered to see the first rehearsals in which the Gold State Coach made its appearance. The coach, dating from 1762, contained panels by Cipriani 'crowded with improprieties' as Horace Walpole put it.[93] It was said to have first been used at the coronation of George IV in 1821, though the historian David Thomas has pointed out that it appears in no contemporary illustrations. It has certainly been used every time since the coronation of William IV. It had not been seen in procession since it conveyed King George and Queen Elizabeth to the State Opening of Parliament in November 1938.

During the war, in 1941, it was spirited away to Mentmore, the Earl of Rosebery's Buckinghamshire estate, on a road journey planned to avoid low bridges. There it was guarded day and night by a team organised by the staff of the National Portrait Gallery. Despite this, it suffered damage and needed extensive restoration. The worn old wheels were made more regular and round, new rubber tyres were put on and flourescent lighting introduced so that the Queen and Prince Philip could be seen.

The coach weighs over four tons and needs eight Windsor Greys to pull it. Four were ridden, there were six walking footmen and a brakesman walked behind it. The coach also contained supports so that the Queen did not have to hold the orb and sceptre on the long procession back to the Palace.

On rehearsal day the coach left the Palace at 6.30am, arrived at Westminster Abbey on the dot of 7 am and made the return journey between 8 and 10 am. In one rehearsal a landau swerved when a horse pulling it stepped over a trace. A Royal Artillery trooper hurt his hand trying to calm the horse. Horses in the procession coped as best they could with admirals, men of the sea, for whom riding was a novel experience.

Ten Clarences were needed for the Commonwealth Prime Ministers. The Royal Mews could only provide five and so five more were loaned by the film producer, Sir Alexander Korda. Horses, some loaned by private individuals, arrived at the Royal Mews in order to start being trained on 21 April 1953. They were destined to make their way to Woolwich experiencing the kind of conditions they would encounter on coronation day. The cheering of thousands of schoolchildren was considered likely to be their severest test. Private owners also stepped forward offering coachmen, harnesses and other equipment. The procession of Clarences was rehearsed at Woolwich Barracks.

The coronation fly-past lined up at Biggin Hill for their rehearsal and flew in massed formation. The decorations continued to go up. When stands were erected outside Westminster Abbey, the canvas was wound round the existing tall trees, giving the impression that the trees were growing through the stands. Some days before the coronation, a 31-year-old stateless man was grateful to be able to sleep under one of the stands until he was arrested and charged with 'wandering about and lodging in the open air.'[94]

A statue of Oliver Cromwell near the Houses of Parliament was completely boxed in for the day so that he was not in evidence on this particularly royal occasion. Crush barriers were mounted at appropriate places.

David Eccles, the Minister of Works, held a press conference, speaking from a desk behind a giant model of the Coronation route. Details of the ceremony with historical precedents were published in numerous supplements.

* * * * *

The Duke of Norfolk now took centre stage inside the Abbey. He would stand at the steps of the throne in his morning coat, wearing his coronet and contrived 'almost alone, to look as though he never wore anything else.'

Young Winston Churchill, grandson of the Prime Minister, had been invited by Lord Portal to be his page, in the hope that he would enjoy a good view of the ceremony. His duty was to carry Portal's coronet. He was excited as it meant at least three days off school, though his uniform would cost £200. At the first rehearsal he observed the Duke of Norfolk in action:

> Though short of stature and ruddy of face and, viewed from across the great expanse of the Abbey, looking like nothing so much as Mr McGoo, the Duke of Norfolk, trailing a long microphone lead behind him, instantly asserted his authority over the proceedings by the brusqueness of his commands but, above all, by the precise knowledge of every detail of the ceremony.[95]

Young Churchill was fascinated to hear the Duke call out: 'Archbishop! Pray bring the crown!' and then: 'Archbishop! That is the wrong crown! Pray bring St Edward's Crown!' The effect on the assembled company was electric. Naturally the young page-to-be had been sent for a haircut in advance of the coronation but this did not stop Field Marshal Mongomery from accosting him: 'Boy! Tell your mother to get your hair cut before the day!'[96]

Behind the scenes the Duke was assisted by Sir George Bellew, Garter King of Arms, the senior Officer at the College of Arms. Garter produced a confidential book for those taking part, subtitled *Ceremonial Detail: Notes and Plans*. It declared that it did not intend to show how the ceremonies *would* be performed, but how they *may* be performed: 'There are several movements which are complex, and time at rehearsals, and even hesitation on the day, may be saved if study of them is made beforehand.'

There were so many people performing different tasks that many of them were moving about at the same time, one official beginning to advance as another retreated. Otherwise the service would have lasted many hours longer. Reassuringly, the book proclaimed: 'What is planned on paper often turns out differently in practice: but, according to these plans, there should be no need for haste, no confusion of movement, and plenty of room in which to move and manoeuvre.'[97]

The book outlined the sequence of movements with a brief summary for each. There followed a map of the Abbey with precise measurements, and about 100 diagrams showing the movement of every figure from the Queen and the Archbishop to the chaplains and pages – the Recognition part of the ceremony alone required 17 such maps. Perhaps the most complicated was the third of 13 maps covering the anointing. Here there is a note: 'There should be no collision if all move at the same pace; the [Lord] Great Chamberlain, for example, is behind everyone else and so, although he crosses their paths, he has a clear way: as does the Sword.'[98]

There were twelve daily rehearsals inside Westminster Abbey from 14 to 29 May. Various issues arose. The Regalia bearing peers were particularly full of demands. Lord Hastings told the Archbishop it was quite wrong for them to be moving towards the altar on the way in while the Queen was kneeling at her faldstool in private devotion. When the Archbishop protested, Hastings said: 'Well we wish to make it quite clear that we think it utterly wrong.' The Archbishop said: 'Well, the Queen must decide.' To this they said: 'We hope that you will represent that this is the wish of the Regalia peers.' But then Lord Portal said: 'Will you please say that it is by no means unanimous and for my part I agree with the view the Archbishop has expressed: it is most right that while the Queen is at her devotion the public attention should be removed from her to follow the delivery of the Regalia.'

When the Queen came to the first rehearsal, the Archbishop asked her and without hesitation she took his side. 'So that is that,' wrote Fisher. 'And I shall have great pleasure in telling the peers concerned at the next rehearsal.'[99]

The Regalia peers were all a certain age. Some recalled that in 1937 it had been

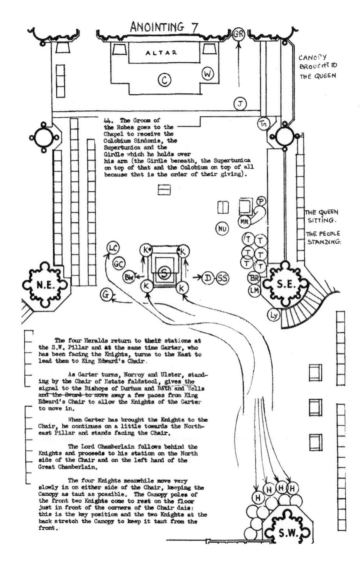

A page from the book produced by Sir George Bellew showing the sequence of movements throughout the Coronation. This page is of the Anointing.

hard to kneel through the communion part with nothing to kneel against. It was agreed that they would only kneel after the Prayer of Humble Access, and that Lord Salisbury, with his bad back, would lower the Sword of State with its point to the ground as an act of reverence.

Soon after this, the Archbishop was pleased when the Duke of Edinburgh suggested that he might make an offering at the time of the communion. In an almost Trollopian situation, Fisher was nervous that anything given at an Abbey service would have to remain part of their collection even though they were 'wealthy in plate of all kinds'[100] and nor was he wrong. He had hoped that the Duke's gift might go to Lambeth Palace chapel which was being restored after wartime bombing and possessed nothing. The Duke solved the problem by offering a silver gilt wafer box to the Abbey and a chalice and paten for Lambeth, in case, he wrote, the Dean got hold of the box.

At the last rehearsal Lord Lyon King of Arms (Sir Thomas Innes of Learney) fainted. A chorister remembered: 'There was a terrible thump and everyone looked round to find that Lyon King-at-Arms had fainted and fallen flat, looking rather like a court card on the carpet, poor man.'[101] The Dean of Westminster, always a shrewd observer, confirmed this:

> The official dress rehearsal took place on Friday 29 May, at 10 am. It dragged at one or two points, notably just before the Anointing when the canopy was being brought during the singing of *Zadok The Priest*; but, generally speaking, it went well. The only untoward incident was the fainting of Lord Lyon, who crashed to the golden carpet with a resounding thud. But fortunately he recovered rapidly and was able to take his place on the Coronation Day.[102]

At the same rehearsal, Lord Simonds, the Lord Chancellor, put on his coronet, which had been designed to be worn over his wig. Without the wig on this occasion, the coronet slipped down to the bridge of his nose. The cartoonist, Osbert Lancaster, caught the mood with a sketch of an elderly tweeded Earl followed by a not much younger man telling an official: 'And ye needn't worry about young Cuthbert knowing the ropes – he's been me page at every Coronation since Edward VII.'[103]

"And ye needn't worry about young Cuthbert
knowing the ropes – he's been me page at
every Coronation since Edward VII!"

The Duchess of Norfolk stood in for the Queen at most of the rehearsals. She was even crowned in King Edward's Chair but of course with a replica crown. The Archbishop found her 'very cool and collected', picking up what she had to do very quickly.[104] Fisher welcomed the Duchess's prompting. For the actual crowning, the trick was to place the front edge where it ought to go on the middle of the forehead, then press it back and down before giving the front a little extra push. The Duchess would tell him: 'A little more forward, a little further down at the back',[105] and the Archbishop rued the fact that on the day the Queen would not be able to assist him in that way. However, the Queen did say that she was prepared to risk the microphones and reassure him or instruct him and say 'all right' when and if it was indeed all right.[106]

The Duchess of Norfolk compared favourably to the Dowager Duchess of Devonshire, as Mistress of the Robes, of whom the Archbishop wrote that she did not help 'by being always a bit vague and apparently much more concerned in getting her own movements right than seeing she was fitting into the general picture, but in the end she got it straight.' He also found that the four Knights of the Garter needed a lot of rehearsing.

The Queen herself attended several rehearsals, sometimes as a spectator and sometimes taking part. One day the Archbishop had a talk with her as she sat contentedly in King Edward's Chair. She told the Archbishop she was reading the little book of devotions which he had prepared for her each day and was so happy to have it. On 19 May the Duke of Edinburgh was there in the morning and she was there for two hours in the afternoon.

During one rehearsal the Duchess of Norfolk stood in for one of the Assistant Bishops and walked beside the Queen guiding her through each step. 'Throughout the whole rehearsal she [the Queen] was at her absolute best,' noted the Archbishop, 'sincere, gay, happy, intensely interested asking all the right questions about her movements and carrying them out very naturally and impressively.'[107] The Queen asked that the real St Edward's Crown be brought for a trial crowning but was told that it was still not ready after eight months of cleaning. So she was crowned with a dummy version of the Imperial State Crown which was far too big.

Another matter that arose was whether or not the Queen should curtsey each time she was greeted at the Recognition. Garter King of Arms was deeply upset when he heard that she might do that, judging: 'In all affairs of state the Sovereign is a man.'[108] He had sleepless nights over the matter and sent the Archbishop 'an urgent letter … saying that 'the whole thing offended him deeply.'[109] He argued: 'Of the 100,000,000 people who will see it on film or television, a proportion may perhaps see something in it akin to 'comic opera'. Others might see in it a sign of weakness – a sign of the final surrender of the Monarchy.' Garter wanted nothing more than an inclination of the head.[110]

Fisher consulted Lord Salisbury who judged that a curtsey was a courtesy. He then told Garter that he would put it to the Queen personally. 'You must advise her rightly,' said Garter. Fisher noted privately: 'I shall certainly advise her in the sense that Garter would call wrong.'[111]

On 27 May when the Queen and Duke came to the Abbey, the Archbishop asked the Queen what she wanted. He recorded the following exchange:

Queen: 'Oh I think a curtsey.'

Duke of Edinburgh: 'Oh no, that is all wrong – you ought not to curtsey to your subjects.'

Queen: 'Well, I do when I open Parliament, and I do not see why I should not. It is as was said a courtesy.'

Duke of Edinburgh (rather unwillingly): 'Well, perhaps that does make a difference.'

Queen: 'I am quite sure.'

Archbishop: 'That Ma'am is a firm ruling is it?'

Queen: 'Yes.'

Fisher saw Garter King of Arms later: 'He was completely unrepentant. However, a half-curtsey was accepted all round.'[112]

At one of the last rehearsals the Bishop of London tried to hand over the Paten and the Moderator forgot to take the Bible back. The Garter Knights did not get moving quickly enough, Lord Ancaster (with St Edward's Staff) was deemed a little slow and the Archbishop was criticised for rubbing the oil off too violently. It was noted that Lord Mowbray needed 'tuning up' at the homage, and that when Lord Salisbury knelt (holding the Sword of State) he needed help to get up. The Gold Staff Officers were too prominent and were told to 'make themselves scarce' and on account of TV and filming, the congregation was urged not to talk or move about when the procession out of the Abbey was forming up.

Various figures were admitted to the full dress rehearsal. James Lees-Milne thought it a 'magnificent spectacle', preferring court dress to the 'overdressed Highland uniforms with too much jabot and too many daggers and horn bugles'. He thought the Duchess of Norfolk 'excellent' and marvelled at how she balanced the heavy orb and sceptre in either hand (though they may not have been so heavy, being replicas like the crown). He continued:

> Nearly all the males were bald. The strong arc lights were unkind to faces and pates, though flattering to the robes. The most striking figure was the Dowager Duchess of Devonshire in red velvet, wearing an enormous diamond tiara and small coronet, a heavy train of infinite length, and long white gloves.[113]

As an official artist who would also photograph the Royal Family back at the

Palace, Cecil Beaton was also allowed into the Abbey for this rehearsal. Despite having seen numerous depictions of previous coronations, he was impressed by the way the chief figures moved, their gestures and 'the whole inspiring poetry of the service, the heavenly music, so clear, so touching to the heart, both its pathos & its joyfulness.'[114]

Beaton was struck by the visual impact of the colour scheme with its reds, gold and smoke blue, and was fascinated by the unexpected effects: 'a page coming to rescue a coronet wearing a turquoise uniform, the Queen exchanging her crimson robe for a Byzantine bell like garment that has come from the Ravenna mosaics, then into a purple velvet robe & train ... Black Rod makes way for a messenger, a mote of light catches a gold sequin on the trainbearer's white satin dress, or on a diamond in the enormous fender tiara of the Mistress of the Robes or a jewel in a Bishop's ring'

Beaton noted that the microphones picked up a lot: 'When the canopy with the gold cloth was brought by the 4 Knights of the Garter we could hear the metallic cloth scraping onto the back of King Edward's Chair with a wheezing noise.' [115]

* * * * *

London was filling up with coronation sightseers. Not everyone enjoyed it. Noël Coward became irritated: 'London is becoming increasingly hellish, swarms of people and a perpetual misery of traffic congestion. The streets are chaos owing to the Coronation decorations. It will be a comfort when it is all over.'[116]

29,200 troops had by now gathered in London and were variously housed in 3,200 tents in Kensington Gardens and in the exhibition buildings of Earl's Court and Olympia. Major-General Julian Gascoigne, GOC London District and Major-General commanding Household Brigade, was in charge of them. 26,700 of these came from the United Kingdom, 2,000 from the Commonwealth and 500 from the Colonies. 1,250 men would march in the procession to the Abbey, and 9,400 on the way back (excluding bands).

Brigadier R.W. Jelf, Commander, 99th AA Brigade, RA, ran the camp for 8,000 at Earl's Court with its basement and three floors, sixty-five staircases and thirteen miles of passages and stairways. Jelf was delighted to be offered the special flat at Earl's Court, normally assigned to VIPs. Anticipating considerable luxuries, he was disappointed to find it was a room 'as bare as a cell' and so his 'dreams of entertaining [his] friends in Hollywood style were never fulfilled.'[117] The camp was made ready and between 29 and 30 May the 8,000 troops arrived, bearing only one suitcase or kitbag each. There were numerous rehearsals of both the 'to' and 'from' processions.

Final fittings were given to the dresses of the peeresses and other ladies. Monsieur Pierre, the Parisian hairdresser, flew in to his shop in Hay Hill to attend to the ladies' hair. He coiffed two pins into some of the ladies' hair to make sure that coronets did not slip on shorter hair than had been the norm at earlier coronations. One of his clients was the Duchess of Kent who left her coronet behind in its black tin box. It was collected later.[118] Again Osbert Lancaster captured the mood with Maudie Littlehampton ordering provisons at a groceries counter in (probably) Fortnum's: 'You know – the size which fits into an earl's coronet and still leaves room for a packet of biscuits and an apple!'[119]

On Sunday 31 May there were large crowds to see the Queen and Duke driven the short journey to the Queen's Chapel, Marlborough House, for matins. Later

" You know – the size which fits into an earl's coronet and
still leaves room for a packet of biscuits and an apple!"

that evening the Archbishop said prayers with the Queen and the Duke and gave them his blessing. He recorded 'a feeling of complete mutual trust free of all kind of constraint and I felt that the Queen and I were entirely in step for the Coronation itself.'[120]

The day before the coronation, £30,000 of jewels were stolen from the Wilton Crescent home of the Duke and Duchess of Sutherland. Detectives were still making enquiries when the Duke and Duchess left for the Abbey the next day.[121]

Key figures in the arrangements of the coronation were honoured just before the ceremony. Princess Margaret and Princess Marie Louise, a surviving granddaughter of Queen Victoria, were given the GCVO and invested in time to wear the new ribbon on the day, GCVOs also being given to the Lord Great Chamberlain, Lord Alanbrooke, Sir David Maxwell-Fyfe and the Archbishop of Canterbury. Many others were honoured.

On 1 June a closed van drew up at Westminster with a police car as escort. The Regalia were brought from the offices of the Goldsmiths and Silversmiths (where they had been for cleaning and general overhaul). They were deposited in the Jerusalem Chamber at 7.45 am. Eight Yeomen Warders guarded them, sleeping in the Jericho Chamber. By tradition the Earl Marshal commandeers the Abbey for the coronation, promising to return the Abbey to the Dean of Westminster after the service in the same condition as he had taken it. Therefore, at 7 pm that evening, the Dean handed over the keys of the Abbey to the Earl Marshal in the presence of Scotland Yard officers.

Thousands of people spent the night in the Mall, oblivious to the showers and even sleet in order to see the processions. Impromptu tents were set up, umbrellas fastened together, while entertainers kept spirits high by playing accordions, banjos and trumpets. Lady Diana Cooper wandered out to have a look at them: 'the Belsen camp of happy sufferers – giant French letters spread over them, sou'westers, Everest equipment.'[122]

Roads were closed from midnight on 1 June until midnight the following day. Coronation day finally arrived.

Coronation Day

The Maids of Honour, a sketch by Cecil Beaton.

THE DAY BEGINS

Very early on the morning of 2 June 8,000 troops were marshalled for action. But the public address system failed to reach the Foot Guards, who 'continued to be regaled by the BBC dance band going full blast.'[1] However, all were out with thirty seconds to spare. The route was lined by street liners between 7.30 and 8 am.

At Westminster Abbey, the choir boys were up at 5 am, over-stimulated by the general excitement and a pillow fight the preceding evening. They were armed with sandwiches, apples and barley sugars to sustain them throughout the service, but most had eaten the lot before the first note was sung. Ticket holders were allowed to outside stands from 6 am, and between 6 and 8 am seat holders had to arrive inside the Abbey. The doors would close at 8.30 sharp. A special underground train transported peers and MPs to Westminster.

Richard Dimbleby, the BBC commentator, had been in the Abbey since 5.30 am. Sitting in his perch in the triforium, he felt he was seeing history in the making. As the figures began to arrive, 'the whole pageant on the floor of the Abbey moved with a slow irresistible rhythm that seemed to lift it out of time altogether.'[2] Dimbleby would be at work for 17 hours.

At 8 Pelham Place Cecil Beaton awoke early: 'The birds had started to sing & the sky was pale grey & already a few electric lights were on in the bedrooms of the houses opposite. An angry wind blew the branches of the cherry tree in the next door garden & gusts of rain were adding to the gloomy scene.' On his arrival at the Abbey Beaton noted that the Gold Staff Officers stationed in the Cloisters were 'blue with cold.'[3]

The Archbishop of Canterbury said matins in the chapel at Lambeth Palace including a prayer for the Queen. He then robed and was driven to the Abbey. His arrival at the annexe was greeted by a great cheer from the waiting crowd.

All over Britain fantastic news arrived to add to the excitement of the day.

A message was received by *The Times* announcing that the New Zealander, E.P. Hillary, and Sherpa Tensing Bhutia had reached the summit of Mount Everest on 29 May. They had attained the ultimate goal of 29,002 feet.

It was their second attempt, an earlier one on 25 May having failed. The climb had been sponsored by the Royal Geographical Society, and most of the team under the leadership of Colonel H.C.J. Hunt, had left England in mid February, establishing a base camp at Thyangboche, Nepal on 26 March. They acclimitised themselves and trained, made a camp on the Khumbu Glacier by 16 April and targetted themselves to make the assault on 15 May. But bad weather, heavy snowfalls and illness amongst the climbers delayed them. After the summit had been reached, it took a while for the dispatch runners to make the long journey from the mountain to Katmandu. But, as *The Times* recorded: 'The suspense has been rewarded, if only by the apt timing of the announcement of this great achievement on the eve of the Coronation.'[4] The apt timing may have been a trifle artificial. The news was held back till 2 June for maximum effect.

* * * * *

Early on coronation morning the Dean's first duty was to take the Imperial State Crown into St Edward's Chapel and leave it there until the Queen needed it at the end of the service. The first duty of the clergy was to fill the Ampulla with holy oil and lay it on the high altar of Westminster Abbey, alongside the Spoon. The oil had proved a problem. Some had been saved from the coronation of George VI but had been lost in flames when the Deanery was bombed in the Blitz (a fact that had been kept secret at the time).

Fortunately the family of the late chemist, Sir P.W. Squire, still retained a tiny phial of it. This was prepared and duly consecrated. The formula dated back to the seventeenth century and included orange flower, oils of roses and of cinnamon, musk, civet, ambergris, oils of jasmine and sesame and flowers of benzoin. It had an unusual fragrance and was amber coloured. Time deepened the colour and mellowed the fragrance.

THE OUTSIDE PROCESSIONS

In the preceding days distinguished figures had descended on London from all parts of the world. Now they converged on Westminster Abbey, each one arriving at a pre-set time in perfect order to be received and escorted to their place.

The Lord Mayor processed from Mansion House at 7.55 am, the Speaker of the House of Commons at 9.30 am. At 9.15 Princess Alice, Countess of Athlone watched the Colonial Rulers set off in four carriages, including 'the statuesque figure' of Queen Salote of Tonga, who weighed in at 20 stone:

> We noticed with curiosity and admiration how she manoueuvred herself into her carriage and then sat down plumb in the middle of the seat of honour. A small but magnificently attired Sultan who had been assigned to the same coach attempted to take his place beside her, but she put out her arm and majestically waved him into the seat facing her.[5]

A procession of ten cars bore certain members of the Royal Family – the Harewoods, the Marchioness of Carisbrooke, the Ramsays, Lady Mountbatten and her daughter Pamela, the Abel Smiths from the Palace at 8.40 am; while more motor-cars conveyed representatives (royal and other) from St James's Palace at 8.50 (including figures such as the Crown Prince of Norway and Mr Malik of the USSR). There were five separate processions on the way to the Abbey, but all five united on the way back.

There were the Commonwealth Prime Ministers grateful for the loan of Alexander Korda's five carriages, including Dr Borg Olivier, won over by a wily Churchill and then Churchill himself, tired on the day, wishing he were in a car, but dressed as a Knight of the Garter, with Lady Churchill in the robes of a Dame Grand Cross of the Order of the British Empire at his side.

Three carriages conveyed the principal members of the Royal Family – the

Princes and Princesses of the Blood Royal, including a granddaughter of Queen Victoria, Lady Patricia Ramsay (formerly Princess Patricia of Connaught, who had renounced her royal titles on marriage in 1919 but reverted to her former style and purple train for this day). The Duchess of Gloucester had been up since 5 am at St James's Palace, 'getting the boys dressed in their new kilts and coats and my husband and I in our robes and orders.'[6]

Peers and peeresses gathered in Westminster Hall before entering the Abbey. 'Chips' Channon observed that 'All was comfortably, smoothly arranged (even the traffic arrangements had been excellent and there was no delay getting there).'[7] Wonderful uniforms and colourful robes abounded. C.L. Sulzberger of *The New York Times* observed: 'Hardly a soul entering the Abbey doors today looks as if she had stepped in from the humdrum twentieth century world.'[8] Inside the Abbey 'Chips' Channon looked about him and noted: 'the front row of 13 Duchesses was a splendid sight.'[9]

At 10 am the procession of Queen Elizabeth The Queen Mother left Clarence House. There was a state landau with her suite, the First Division, Captain's Escort of the Household Cavalry; then she and Princess Margaret travelled in the Glass Coach, followed by the Second Division of the Captain's Escort with Standard.

Inside Westminster Abbey, everyone waited in anticipation of the arrivals. Lady Diana Cooper was relieved to find herself well placed and with a good view:

> The theatre was *brilliantly* lit from nowhere – it had to be, because of TV, but it suited the stained glass, playing–card primary-colour realness, and in compensation for those who might find it blatant, not a photographer not a lens not a flash was to be seen, even Cecil B. in the rafters was invisible ...[10]

Iain Tennant was one of the Royal Company of Archers on duty as an usher and wearing their uniform. Amongst his responsibilities he had to look after Sir Winston Churchill and Dr Malan of South Africa. Forewarned that Malan might need a lavatory during the service, he made himself known. The South African President became distinctly peppery and told him he could find his own way. 'And if you think I am too old to last four hours, you're wrong.'[11] He did not go.

Presently Iain Tennant sat down on some steps by the choir stalls and as he did so his trousers split up the back. A nearby peeress said to him: 'If you want a needle and thread, I have one on my coronet.'[12]

Before the service, the litany was sung and then at 9.55 the Dean of Westminster, the prebendaries and the Abbey choir processed from the altar to the Great West Door, conveying the Regalia to the annexe. They arrived at 10.10 am, consigned the pieces into the care of the Lord Chamberlain's Office and these were placed on the special table. Presently the Regalia were delivered by the Comptroller of the Lord Chamberlain's Office to the Lord High Constable's representative who in turn gave them to the Lord Great Chamberlain (the Marquess of Cholmondeley).

The carriages deposited their charges at the west end of the Abbey and the internal processions were formed. Channon found the long wait 'enthralling as every few minutes a procession of distinguished guests, relations, minor royalties entered and were escorted to their seats.'[13] Cecil Beaton was especially intrigued by Princess Marie Louise, 'wonderfully old & angry with her silly vulgar lady-in-waiting' who could not control her train and by Princess Andrew of Greece, who had arrived by car.[14] Her family were amused that she had had a special full-length nun's robe run up for her in Paris. She stood out by her simplicity.

Some 260 people processed within the Abbey. Channon thought the Duchess of Kent 'fairy-like, and there was a well-bred gasp as she walked in with her children.'[15] Cecil Beaton, on the other hand, judged the Duchess: 'very stolid not graceful, her daughter [Princess Alexandra] inept in a soft dress not a bit pretty & getting into difficulties when her attendant gave her her train; Princess Royal a splendid war horse; Princess Margaret well poised.'[16]

Lady Diana Cooper was disappointed by Princess Margaret: 'wings clipped by the King's death, not all glorious within, rather dusky and heavy featured,'[17] while Channon matched the arrivals against his memories of 1937: 'Queen Mum was OK, but compared badly with Queen Mary's entry last time.'[18]

In due course the Archbishops (in their copes and mitres) and Bishops Assistant joined the procession to await the arrival of the Queen.

THE STATE PROCESSION

The State Procession, which was the Queen's procession, was led by a sole officer of the War Office Staff and left Earl's Court at 8.56. He was followed by troopers of the Household Cavalry, Guards bands, detachments of foot guards, the King's Troop, Royal Artillery, chaplains and ADCs first of the RAF, then the Army and then the Navy. There were over 1,000 guardsmen in the procession. Then came Air Ministry, War Office and Admiralty Staff, senior officers of the Armed Forces of the Commonwealth and increasingly senior figures in Northern Ireland District and Home Command.

Carriages conveyed the Marshals of the Royal Air Force, men such as Sir Arthur (Bomber) Harris, Lord Douglas of Kirtleside and Lord Tedder and one elderly Field Marshal – Lord Wilson of Libya. Four Field Marshals rode on horseback: Sir Claude Auchinleck, Earl Alexander of Tunis, Lord Ironside and Viscount Montgomery of Alamein (who was later spotted sitting in the annexe in his Garter robes reading about Hillary and Everest in *The Times*). More carriages conveyed the Admirals of the Fleet, including Sir John Cunningham, Lord Chatfield and the Earl of Cork and Orrery. Members of the service Councils followed and the UK Chiefs of Staff.

Just before the Gold State Coach came the Queen's Escort from the Colonial and Commonwealth Contingents, the Yeomen of the Guard, the Watermen and others, various ADCs and the Commissioner of the Metropolitan Police.

The Queen and Duke left Buckingham Palace in the State Coach, pulled by eight Greys at 10.26, alongside which rode the Master of the Horse (the Duke of Beaufort), the Lord High Constable (Field Marshal Viscount Alanbrooke), the Captain of the Yeomen of the Guard (the Earl of Onslow), Gold Stick-in-Waiting (Major-General Sir Richard Howard-Vyse), the Field Officer in Brigade Waiting (Colonel T.F.C. Winnington) and the Silver Stick-in-Waiting (Colonel E.J.S. Ward).

After the State Coach came the Standard, and then on horseback, the Personal

ADCs to the Queen – Vice-Admiral Earl Mountbatten of Burma and HRH The
Duke of Gloucester. Mountbatten apparently made an enormous fuss wishing to
ride alongside the carriage. The Queen put him firmly in his place. There were
various further ADCs and Equerries (one of whom was Viscount Althorp – later
Earl Spencer and father of the future Diana, Princess of Wales), three royal grooms
and two further Divisions of the Sovereign's Escort.

THE ENTRANCE INTO THE ABBEY

The Gold State Coach arrived at the Annexe of the Abbey at exactly 11 am. The
Queen alighted, wearing the coronation dress, the crimson velvet Parliamentary
train and the King George IV diadem.

As he had informed the media at one of his press conferences, it was the Duke
of Norfolk's 'honour' as Earl Marshal to receive the Queen. He was there in his
ancient ducal robes, wearing the Collar of the Order of the Garter. This was not
the first time he had shaken the Queen's hand at a coronation. He had been at
a similar entrance in May 1937 when she arrived as a little girl for her father's
coronation.

The Queen's anticipated arrival had the congregation in a state of intense
expectation. There was a sudden 'uproar from nowhere'[19] which prompted the
entire congregation to rise to their feet in unison. They thought the Queen had
arrived, only to be confronted by a troupe of carpet sweepers undertaking a last
minute sweep. There was a ripple of laughter and everyone sat down again.

A guard of honour of The Queen's Company, Grenadier Guards, was in
the Vestibule and the Queen's Company Colour was posted at the entrance of
the Choir. Peers who had been in the outside procession such as the Duke of
Gloucester, 'very solemn & large'[20], made their way to their seats. The Duke of
Edinburgh put on his ducal robes and took his place in the Queen's procession
as did the peers carrying the Regalia. Lady Diana Cooper noted: 'Ducal husband:
bigger, better, newer robes than the others, padded to a François I width by

admiral's epaulettes.'[21]

Audrey Russell was one of the BBC commentators with a vantage point overlooking the arrivals at the Great West Door. She had been involved in many rehearsals and was aware that a tiny piece of red thread had been stitched into the blue carpet ten yards from the Great West Door. This was an important marker. It would take the Queen exactly 55 seconds to walk from that spot to the Gothic Archway, so that was the point at which her wireless commentary was to end and the State Trumpeters were to sound their fanfare. To her horror, Audrey Russell noticed a young Gold Staff Officer kneel down and snip the red ribbon away.

In the annexe the Queen turned to the six Maids of Honour who would carry her train and asked: 'Ready girls?' Audrey Russell waited nervously, but everyone was well rehearsed and the fanfares sounded exactly as the Queen reached the point where the ribbon should have been. Off they went at 11.15.

Parry's magnificent anthem, *I was glad,* was sung by the massed choirs as the Queen processed up the the full length of the main aisle. Cecil Beaton watched her:

And then the Queen, her demeanour of childish simplicity & humility, with pink hands folded in front, in contrast to the grandeur of her heavily encrusted dress, her hair tightly curled, the Victorian crown perched straighter on her head than usual, & the effect thus even better, her cheeks very pink.'[22]

The Dean of Westminster wrote:

For the next two hours or more everything passed off without any hitch worth mentioning. The Queen did her part perfectly with great recollectedness and simplicity, and without any outward trace of nervousness or self-consciousness. The Mistress of the Robes and the Maids of Honour were dignified and graceful, and moved with notable precision.[23]

There were of course a few minor faults. The Queen reached the Amphitheatre. She had rehearsed the genuflection to the altar many times, but on the day she forgot it. Few noticed this at the time.

Throughout the service the Queen was assisted by her two supporting Bishops.

The Dean again noted:

> The supporting Bishops – Durham [Michael Ramsey, later Archbishop of
> Canterbury], aged under fifty [48] and looking venerable as a septuagenarian, and
> Bath and Wells [Harold Bradfield], not good looking but full of solicitude for the
> Queen – performed their evolutions with conspicuous skill. The Archbishop of
> Canterbury (who has it in his power to make or mar a Coronation) rose to the
> occasion nobly. His voice was clear, his articulation unaffected, and his mastery of
> detail complete ...[24]

But Lord Cunningham of Hyndhope, prominent as Lord High Steward, was not
impressed by the Bishops in general, giving them 'low marks for their proficiency
in ceremonial skill' and disappointed that they needed to be prompted during the
service.[25]

The Queen took her place in the Chair of Estate on the south side of the Altar.
As agreed, the peers carrying the Regalia continued forward while she knelt in
prayer. They handed the Regalia to the Dean who in turn laid them on the altar.
At 11.30 the great Coronation service began. It continued until 1.45 pm.

THE RECOGNITION

The Recognition was the first part of the service and involved the Archbishop,
the Lord Chancellor, the Lord Great Chamberlain and the Lord High Constable.
The Archbishop had stressed the importance of the Recognition as the symbolic
chance for the congregation to identify the person presented to them for anointing
and crowning. The congregation needed to be sure that they were getting the right
monarch.

The Archbishop presented the new Queen to the East, South, West and
North sides of the Abbey, and each time the same shout of response rang out.
The Archbishop intoned: 'Sirs, I here present unto you Queen Elizabeth, your
undoubted Queen, wherefore all you who are come this day to do your homage
and service. Are you willing to do the same?' This was answered with the shout:

'God Save Queen Elizabeth' and a fanfare of trumpets.

The Queen acknowledged these cheers with the agreed slight curtsey. The Archbishop judged this 'not only most suitable but absolutely captivating in its grace,'[26] while James Lees-Milne watched on television: 'It was a gesture on her part of obeisance and yet tremendous majesty – the only occasion she will ever be known to curtsey.'[27]

Lawrence Tanner, at work as a Gold Staff Officer, also commended the Queen's 'mixture of grace, charm, dignity and humility' as she curtsied after being presented as 'Your undoubted Queen'.[28]

THE OATH

The Queen returned to her chair and the oath was then administered obliging her to solemnly promise to govern all her Peoples, uphold the laws of God and maintain the Protestant Reformed Religion. Preceded by the Sword of State the Queen went to the altar, laid her hand on the bible and said: 'The things which I have here promised, I will perform and keep. So help me God.'

There had been a great deal of discussion as to how to amend the oath to recognise the Commonwealth. In the end it remained more or less as before because Lord Swinton, the Colonial Secretary, ruled out changes that would need every Commonwealth country's agreement, something he was not confident that he could obtain.

THE PRESENTING OF THE HOLY BIBLE

Scotland then played its small part in the service, the first time it had done so. The holy bible was presented by the Moderator of the General Assembly with the words: 'Here is wisdom; this is the royal law; these are the lively oracles of God.' The Queen then handed the bible back. After this the communion service began.

THE ANOINTING

The most solemn and important moment of the coronation service now took place – the anointing of the Queen. While the choir sang *Zadok the Priest* the Queen was divested of her crimson robe and wearing a simple white dress over the coronation dress, she moved to King Edward's Chair and took her place there. As previously mentioned, the chair faces the altar not the congregation. Lawrence Tanner observed the Queen 'in the coronation chair, having been disrobed of her crimson robe, clothed in simple white, terribly alone, awaiting her anointing.'[29] And the Dean commented: 'Nothing could match the magnificence of *Zadok the Priest*.'[30]

For this private moment of the service, the television cameras were diverted. The four Knights of the Garter advanced with the canopy, the Earl Marshal disappointed that it sagged in the middle and 'Chips' Channon noting that they 'rather bungled the canopy and were clumsy.'[31]

By long established tradition, as far back as Henry VI, the anointing canopy has been carried by four Knights of the Garter, but they were unlikely to have done so at the coronations of Queen Mary or Queen Elizabeth I. The Order of the Garter took on special prominence in the reign of the first Queen Elizabeth. William IV had four Dukes, who all held the Garter, while in 1902 and 1911 one of the canopy holders was the 5th Earl of Rosebery (1847-1929), one-time Prime Minister. In 1937, the canopy was held by the 7th Marquess of Londonderry, the 3rd Duke of Abercorn, the 2nd Earl of Lytton and 7th Earl Stanhope (the latter two both commemorated in ceramic by Carl Thieme).

In 1953 the canopy holders were the 7th Duke of Portland, the 7th Duke of Wellington, the 5th Earl Fortescue and the 2nd Viscount Allendale, who were amongst the more recent creations in the Order.

For a Queen consort, the canopy has by tradition been carried by four Duchesses.

Very few people could see this part, but the poet John Betjeman, reporting for

A ceramic model of the Earl of Lytton, by Carl Thieme, 1937.

Country Life, watched the Dean, 'a tall, monkish, medieval-looking man' come forward with the gold ampulla, shaped like an eagle, dip a spoon into it and then wait as the Archbishop dipped his thumb into it.[32]

The anointing was a rite of passage. The distinguished historian, L.G. Wickham Legg, had written: 'Nothing which goes before and nothing which follows can approach the anointing in significance. Without it the king cannot receive the royal ornaments, without it, in a word, he is not king.'[33] This is not unlike baptism or confirmation, and is conducted with as much privacy as possible. That done, the more temporal and magnificent side of the ceremony commenced.

At about this point Prince Charles (then styled the Duke of Cornwall), who was not yet five years old, was brought to the Abbey by his nanny, Helen Lightbody, to sit between his grandmother, the Queen Mother, and his aunt, Princess Margaret. Thus he saw the great spectacle before him, and in particular the moment when his mother was crowned.

Prince Charles was dressed in white and wore his Coronation medal (he still wears it when in uniform today). Years later he told his biographer that he only remembered the glorious music and the coronets being put on in unison. He had been annoyed that the Palace barber had cut his hair too short and plastered it to his head 'with the most appalling gunge.'[34] His sister, Princess Anne, was not quite three. To her considerable irritation she had to stay home at the Palace, watching the processions arrive and leave.

After the anointing the Dean and the Mistress of the Robes robed the Queen in the Colobium Sindonis and the Supertunica – or cloth of gold. John Betjeman was impressed by the way they carried out 'this delicate office' in public, making it look 'something beautiful and tender.'[35]

THE PRESENTING OF THE SPURS AND SWORD
AND THE OBLATION OF THE SAID SWORD

The Queen again sat in King Edward's Chair while the Lord Great Chamberlain presented the spurs that as a female sovereign she would not wear. She touched them and they were sent back to the high altar.

Next there was the complicated business of the sword. Lord Salisbury handed the Sword of State to the Lord Chamberlain, swapping it for another sword in its scabbard. This he gave to the Archbishop for blessing. The Archbishop then handed it to the Queen who offered it at the high altar.

Here was the occasion for the only other mistake in the service. As the sword was being redeemed, the Archbishop thought he should now receive the Armills. He soon realised his mistake and panicked, throwing up his arms as if to say: 'What have I done?' Garter King of Arms gave this gesture a generous interpretation later, describing it as a 'charming little blessing that you gave the Queen while the sword was being redeemed.'[36]

THE INVESTING WITH THE ARMILLS,
THE STOLE ROYAL AND THE ROBE ROYAL:
THE DELIVERY OF THE ORB

The Queen was now back in King Edward's Chair. The Dean then gave the Commonwealth Armills to the Archbishop who placed them on the Queen's wrists. The Dean and the Mistress of the Robes attended to the Stole Royal and the Robe Royal, the Lord Great Chamberlain fastening the clasps. And then the Archbishop gave the Queen the orb and she handed it back again. The orb went back to the altar. Writing later, the Dean praised himself for this part, saying that he 'managed to bring the various articles of the Regalia to the Archbishop in the right order at the right time, and contrived with the help of the Mistress of the Robes to vest the Queen at the appropriate moments without bungling.'[37]

But he did not escape criticism entirely. He annoyed the Earl Marshal by not wearing the cope prescribed for him – preferring the Charles II one to the one given specially by the Queen – and later he was to cause some trouble with the alms dish at the communion.[38]

THE INVESTITURE

Per Annulem, et Per Sceptrum et Baculum

Lord Hardinge of Penshurst, a former Private Secretary to King George VI, stood in for the Keeper of the Jewel House (who was unwell) and so it was he who gave the Archbishop the Queen's ring. This was placed on the fourth finger of her right hand. Lord Woolton then came from his nearby seat to present the Glove, and the Queen then received the Sceptre with the Cross and the Rod with the Dove. Each time a new piece of Regalia was given to the Queen, the Archbishop pronounced special words. When he gave her the Rod with the Dove, he said: 'Punish the wicked, cherish the just, and lead your people wherein they should go.'

THE PUTTING ON OF THE CROWN

Now that the Queen had taken the oath, been anointed and received the necessary Regalia, it was at last time for the Archbishop to prepare to crown her. In advance of the ceremony Garter King of Arms had attached a very small gold star to the crown in order to avoid the fumbling and hesitation that had occurred at the 1937 coronation.

For this moment the entire congregation rose. The Archbishop blessed St Edward's Crown on the High Altar. He advanced to the Queen, stretched his arms to their full length and held the crown above her head so that all could see. He then lowered it slowly onto the Queen's head. He described this part in his diary:

> On the day, having placed & adjusted the crown deliberately, I raised my hands clear of the crown and stepped down to the floor and back. As I looked anxiously to see whether it was all right, the Queen gave me a lovely quick smile to convey that it was all right.[39]

The congregation cried out: 'God Save The Queen', and the princes and princesses, peers and peeresses and the Kings of Arms put on their coronets. It was a glorious moment, the white-gloved arms of the peeresses resembling the long necks of swans as they rose in unison. The Abbey resounded with fanfares and loud shouts of acclaim. Outside salutes were fired by artillery at the Tower of London and in Hyde Park to let the crowds know that their Queen was crowned.

'It is a hard moment to capture without hyperbole,' wrote the American columnist C.L. Sulzberger: 'And through the tall gothic windows, over the heads of those determined servants of the crown – the Queen's Field and Air Marshals, Generals, Admirals, and most redoubtable of all, the Queen's Prime Minister, Sir Winston Churchill, came the dull boom of guns from the venerable tower fortress down the Thames.'[40]

Through the medium of television and wireless, this moment like almost all those preceding it, could be shared in most corners of the globe. But there was the odd anti-climax too. Audrey Russell spotted that as the peers put on their coronets, one of them had forgotten that he had used it to hold his sandwiches. 'He heard a soft thud and, looking down, saw a plastic-covered triangular package at his feet'.[41]

Nearby as a page, young Winston Churchill 'could not restrain a sideways glance at the mesmeric beauty of our young Queen. I was amazed that one so slight could bear the weight of the crown – over 4½ lbs – with such apparent ease.'[42]

THE BENEDICTION AND ENTHRONING

The Coronation service continued with the Benediction and Enthroning. The Benediction involved the Archbishops of Canterbury and York and all the Bishops gathered in excellent seats on the north side of the altar opposite the Royal Box. The Queen was escorted to the throne and symbolically 'lifted' into it. She thus took possession of her kingdom. The peers who had carried the Regalia and figures such as the Earl Marshal, the Lord Great Chamberlain and the Home Secretary gathered behind her in a protective phalanx.

THE HOMAGE

For the homage the Queen handed her two sceptres to supporting peers. The Archbishop of Canterbury had won the easy battle to do homage first. He was followed by the Duke of Edinburgh, the first time he had played an independent role in the ceremony. He duly promised to be the Queen's 'liege man of life and limb'. Though he was meant to begin: 'I, Philip, Duke of Edinburgh', he simply said: 'I, Philip'. Lawrence Tanner recalled: 'One who was standing on the steps of the throne told me that he and those around him were so moved that they were almost in tears.'[43]

The Queen's uncle, the Duke of Gloucester, and her young cousin, the Duke of Kent, then did their homage in turn. The young Duke of Kent was terrified that he would forget the lines of his homage, which he had learnt by heart. What no one had told him was that the Bishop of Durham would be holding up a card with the words written on it. After that, the senior peer in each rank of the peerage knelt before the Queen, while the other peers of the same rank remained in their places, but took off their coronets and knelt.

Interestingly all the peers who did homage had done so to George VI, except for the Viscount of Arbuthnott. In 1937 Viscount Hereford, the senior Viscount, had done homage, but in 1953 the new Lord Hereford was only 20 and did not come of age until 4 November, so he missed out.

As previously explained, the Marquess of Winchester was not summoned to the coronation so the Marquesses were represented by the 12th Marquess of Huntly (who had succeeded to the Marquessate in February 1937 not long before the coronation of George VI in May that year). The 21st Earl of Shrewsbury (a godson of George V and Queen Mary) represented the Earls and, as stated, the 14th Viscount of Arbuthnott represented the Viscounts.

The 25th Lord Mowbray, Segrave and Stourton knelt for the Barons, his first barony dating as far back as 1283. Lord Mowbray was given a front row seat in front of the Dukes so that he could emerge easily. His son was a Gold Staff Officer and, before the service, came over to tell him how lucky he was to have such a good seat. 'Lucky? Lucky? My dear boy, these upstart Dukes were still tilling the fields when we were Barons!' This had an electric effect on the Dukes and the Duke of Rutland hid Mowbray's coronet with his sandwiches in it. When years later the Queen was told this story she commented: 'he was being all Grenadierish.'[44]

As the most junior Viscountess, Lady Diana Cooper was sitting next to Mowbray's wife Sheila who became extremely agitated as the moment came for him to do allegiance. 'He'll never manage,' she sighed. 'He has to put his spectacles on to read the oath, and with them he can't see the floor.' Lady Mowbray averted her gaze while Lady Diana observed Lord Mowbray and his 'anxious gathering up of the cloak and the almost crab stampede down.'[45]

When the homages were over, there was a beating of drums and more trumpets and cries of 'God Save Queen Elizabeth – Long Live Queen Elizabeth – May The Queen live forever.'

THE COMMUNION

Next there was the full communion service which began with everyone singing *All People that on Earth do Dwell.* This was a great feature of this coronation, but the Archbishop thought it was 'too dressed in musical elaborations of organ, orchestra, trumpets so that the people did not find it easy to follow the time & came in after each verse.'[46] Like the rest of the service, the hymn was broadcast on speakers outside and those on the stands were encouraged to join the singing.

The Queen took off her crown and again handed over her two sceptres and knelt on the faldstool. For this part of the service the Queen was joined by the Duke of Edinburgh who removed his coronet.

Here was another time when the Dean let the Archbishop down. He had replaced the small basin used at rehearsals with an enormous alms dish which proved unwieldy for the Archbishop to hold. The Archbishop had to have one foot on the step higher and hold it awkwardly at them.[47] The Queen gave her oblation – an altar cloth – and an ignot of gold weighing a pound. Prince Philip found the dish so heavily embossed that, as he said later, he could not find a flat place on which to put his box without it see-sawing to and fro.

This was the other part of the service that was not broadcast. The BBC bowed out for a time after the Prayer of Humble Access with the words: 'Now we come to the most solemn part of the service.' Communion was taken by the Archbishop of Canterbury, the Dean of Westminster and the Bishops Assistant and then given to the Queen and the Duke, the Archbishop giving them the cup and the Dean the bread. There was a muddle after the Archbishop decided to acknowledge the Moderator, who would not be taking the sacrament. 'Feed on him in thy heart by faith with thanksgiving,' he said spontaneously, prompting the Dean to offer him the wine, which the Moderator politely declined. There was an exchange of letters about this later.

The Queen returned to her throne, replaced her crown herself and took back her sceptres. The Duke returned to his chair in front of the peers and put his coronet on once more.

THE RECESS

While a *Te Deum* was sung, the Queen repaired to the area behind the High Altar and went into St Edward's Chapel, preceded by the Archbishop, and accompanied by the Groom of the Robes, the Lord Great Chamberlain, the Lords carrying the Regalia and the Dean of Westminster. There she took off St Edward's Crown, which is exceptionally heavy, and the Robe Royal and instead put on the Imperial State Crown and her train of purple velvet. One of the Bishops offered one of the Maids of Honour a nip of brandy as she had looked faint earlier in the service.

As the Queen left the chapel in the procession that would lead to the Great West Door, two verses of the National Anthem were sung.

Up till now there had been no close-ups of the Queen on television but as she emerged from St Edward's Chapel, the cameras moved closer and closer in. A BBC engineer, Ben Shaw, was waiting in the wings with a button that he could press to eliminate any images that broke the rules. These images broke every rule in the book. Shaw watched and he waited but he did not have the heart to press the button. He served the nation well. The resulting moving pictures of the Queen were stunning, something that modern TV viewers would take for granted, but which were exceptionally special in 1953.

The Queen passed down through the Choir and the Nave and into the annexe to prepare for the long procession through the wet streets of London back to Buckingham Palace. Everyone made their way out in turn. One of the 400 choristers in the Abbey was Anthony Garnett. He enjoyed watching the processions leave: 'The Queen Mother was particularly gracious and lovely, bowing to Sir Winston and other friends and dignitaries. Princess Margaret looked rather shy, and

Princess Marie Louise very frail.'[48] Princess Alice, Countess of Athlone, spotted that as Sir Winston Churchill walked down the aisle, 'he paused to exchange some impish pleasantries with the royal pages.'[49]

Thus ended the coronation service, planned to the last detail over so many months.

* * * * *

The Queen took a short break but soon sent word that she was ready for the procession home, whenever needed. The Duke of Edinburgh suggested to the Archbishop that he should go in and have a word with her.

They discussed the ceremony. The Queen told him that she had been willing him hard not to come out for the Armills before the business with the sword was completed. He mentioned her failure to genuflect and decided they were 'all square.'[50] The Queen told him that he had put the crown on much better than she did when she replaced it herself after the *Glorias*. Fisher found her 'not overtired, deeply content and happy.' They discussed the funny moments in the service:

> Mowbray is certainly the comic piece in the whole procedure. He came down from his homage all over the place, bunching up his robe and tripping over it and, as the Queen said, with moth balls and pieces of ermine flying in all directions.[51]

The Archbishop told the Queen that the Duchess of Norfolk had complained that Mowbray had filthy hands at the rehearsal and that he cut the last rehearsal altogether.

The Queen prepared to re-enter the Gold State Coach.

* * * * *

The Dean of Westminster was pleased with the way it had gone, especially the televising. He was able to go through the service 'quite unconscious of any disturbance and oblivious of the fact that millions of eyes were watching the proceedings':

> The arclights were so sited in the triforium that one was conscious of no dazzle, while at the same time they showed up the brilliance of the golden carpet with which the theatre and sanctuary were covered. Such misgivings as I had had as to the desirability of television and colour filming were entirely allayed, and in the event the advocates of such publicity (within the prescribed limits) were amply justified.[52]

The only hazard had been that his head required powdering from time to time or it would have resembled one of the Abbey's monumental busts and various figures were given pink cheeks and brown foreheads. The Dean concluded:

> The verdict of Dr Jocelyn Perkins [Minor Canon and Sacrist 1900-58], who had attended three previous Coronations, was that the Coronation of Queen Elizabeth II was 'out and away the most impressive of the four'.

> The only blot on an unforgettable day was the weather; but the crowds outside were in great good spirits and enjoyed themselves none the less.[53]

Though not so many survive from that great day, some of the participants recorded their memories. Prince Philip wrote: 'Much of that day remains rather a blur in my memory, although I have the most vivid memories of individual incidents.' The Duke of Kent recalled: 'The ceremony was almost overpowering… I saw it all, but I didn't know who most of the people were. Since then, of course, I have seen the pictures and watched the film and I recognise them…'[54] Princess Alexandra's principal memory was that she envied her cousin, Princess Elizabeth of Yugoslavia's dress from Dior, which she thought much prettier than hers from Hartnell. Their brother, Prince Michael of Kent remembered the Coronation vividly, the fine clothes and the many rehearsals:

> I also remember the spectacle, and how glamorous the Queen was. I was only eleven, but she was stunning, and the whole thing was overwhelming. There was an element of magic, certainly for me.[55]

Harold Macmillan found the ceremony 'very impressive, and in spite of the rain, so was the procession. The enthusiasm of the people has been extraordinary – a sort of outpouring of pent-up emotion.'[56] Lady Diana Cooper concluded: 'It could not have been more moving and true – and touching, because of the size and grace of the central figure.'[57]

'Chips' Channon thought: 'What a day for England, and the traditional forces of the world. Shall we ever see the like again?'[58]

THE DRIVE HOME

The Gold State Coach rolled through the streets of London on an extended journey back to Buckingham Palace.

It was on this drive home when the rain came down in buckets that Queen Salote of Tonga won the hearts of the British by sitting resolutely in an open carriage. Under the robes of the Order of the British Empire, the Queen wore a skirt of tapa, covered with a Tongan apron of plaited grass and a blouse of hibiscus fibre. In her hair she wore red feathers from the neck and breast of the sacred kula bird (the exclusive perquisite of ladies of the Polynesian Royal Houses).[59]

Everyone fell for her, even James Lees-Milne, who described her as 'a vast, brown, smiling bundle with a tall red knitting-needle in her hat (it having begun as a plume of feathers).'[60]

Others found the procession harder. The Duchess of Gloucester wrote that 'the long drive after the ceremony – mostly in the pouring rain – was rather tedious for the boys. We drove in the same carriage as the Princess Royal, who kept them amused with funny stories of past events.'[61]

Princess Alice, Countess of Athlone, shared her carriage with Princess Marie Louise, who had been desperately thirsty and poured herself a generous glass of water and quaffed it down just before they left the Abbey. Unfortunately it was neat gin and went straight to her head. On the drive back, Princess Marie-Louise nearly fell out of the coach and her tiara slipped down as she leaned further out of the window, waving to the crowds.[62] They pressed on, but Sir Winston Churchill found it all too tiring. When his carriage approached Downing Street, he had his carriage turn in and retreated home.

Back at Buckingham Palace the Queen found Cecil Beaton ready with his camera and two different backdrops so that he could set up the royal groups in turn with the minimum waste of time. His magnificent photographs of the Queen, seated in front of a painted backdrop of the Henry VII Chapel and wearing the Imperial State Crown, more than rivalled the rather stiff official portraits by the painter, James Gunn, destined for overseas embassies and Government Houses.

Later in the day the Earl Marshal and the Archbishop looked through the film of the service as the Queen wanted them to have the chance to censor news footage before it was distributed through the country.[63]

The Queen and the Royal Family then appeared on the balcony at Buckingham Palace.

That night Churchill introduced the Queen before her broadcast to the nation. He said: 'The words gracious and noble are words familiar to us all in courtly phrasing. Tonight they have a new ring in them because we know they are true about the gleaming figure whom Providence has brought to us, and brought to us in times where the present is hard and the future veiled.'[64]

Some hours after the ceremony, there was a curious sight that delighted those who saw it – a solitary peer was spotted at St James's Park underground station on his way home, still in full robes and carrying his coronet. He took the tube to Sloane Square.

* * * * *

The coronation was celebrated throughout the Commonwealth. 17 million people took part in local celebrations, 7 million giving their own parties. It had been expensive to put it on, the final cost heading to £1 million, but there were great benefits for Britain. It was said at the time that this compared well to the expenses involved in the election and inauguration of General Dwight D. Eisenhower as

President of the United States, which was nearer £25 million.

Press coverage was generally enthusiastic. *The Guardian* is not a newspaper known for a pro-monarchical position. Harry Boardman, their political correspondent, wrote:

> Others of our Queens, Elizabeth I and Victoria, for example, have swayed the hearts of their people after a time, but Elizabeth II captured them from the start. She has done it not merely in virtue of her youth and grace, but because she joins to these qualities the high seriousness we have come to associate with the House of Windsor. That gravity was hers today, and perfectly attuned to the occasion. It made its subtle appeal to all hearts. It stirred the sense of a young woman set apart and dedicated and even a little lonely and greatly deserving a nation's affection and support.[65]

In the Soviet Republic they hardly reported the coronation at all, but mentioned Mr Malik's presence in the Abbey and his visit to the Foreign Office the next day. A Communist Chinese broadcast mentioned that the Deputy Foreign Minister had attended the coronation reception in Peking and that Mr Chou-En-lai had sent a message of congratulation to Sir Winston Churchill.[66]

All too soon life returned to normal. Osbert Lancaster depicted a large schoolmaster looming over two small boys at a desk: "Now I wonder if Fauntleroy Mi. has sufficiently recovered from his television triumphs at the Abbey to give us the genitive plural of 'mensa'?"[67]

On 9 June the Archbishop wrote to George Barnes, Director of Television at the BBC:

> You know that I am no great supporter of TV, regarding it as an extravagance, and a supreme time waster. But I admit that for certain occasions it is a great benefit. And I freely say that thanks to TV the Coronation Service got into countless homes and brought to the viewers a realization of the Queen's burden, the Queen's dedication, God's presence and God's consecration, of religion and of themselves – which otherwise they would not even have guessed at. I think the religious impact of the Coronation (if I believe half what I am told) has been immense. It is in large measure due to Radio and John Snagge on the one part, and TV and Richard Dimbleby and you and your staff on the other part. It was grand. And the spirit of cooperation

"Now I wonder if Fauntleroy Mi. has sufficiently recovered
from his television triumphs at the
Abbey to give us the genitive plural of 'mensa'?"

among all who had a share in it from the Queen downward made it what it was.[68]

And the next day he replied to a letter from the Duke of Norfolk and congratulated him on his exquisite handling of the whole matter:

> But the greatest treasure (apart from the service itself) was the family cooperation of everybody: and I think that derived in no small measure from the way in which you allowed me to cooperate with you and yourself cooperated with me. For my part, I regard it as one of the happiest collaborations of my life in its operation and in its results.
>
> As you say, it really was great fun as well as being a tremendous occasion. And your kindness and goodwill and the Duchess's have meant a great deal to me.[69]

The Queen thanked the Archbishop for his support before and during the service:

> I find it very difficult to put into words just what it meant to me but your continual encouragement and explanation made the tremendous significance of the service and the strain of that long day so much easier to face. In particular, both Philip and I

would like to thank you for your prayers for us on Trinity Sunday – they gave us both much needed strength and calmness. The little book of Devotions for the month before June 2nd, which you so kindly wrote for us was greatly valued and we are all most grateful to you for enabling us to join all together in thoughts and prayers all leading up to the great day itself.[70]

* * * * *

Within the week the Archbishop of Canterbury preached a sermon at St Paul's Cathedral and said that everyone was still under the spell of the coronation:

Every trend of thought or conversation came back to the wonder of it, the unforgettable bearing of the Queen, to the overwhelming sense of dedication to God, of worship of God, of consecration by God, and of communion with God, which had impressed every one in the Abbey, and had been transferred, without any loss of religious significance, to those listening or viewing.[71]

18,462 people visited Westminster Abbey within two days to see it laid out for the service. They were able to admire the replicas of the crown jewels placed in the annexe.

* * * * *

The Queen was not crowned in any of the Commonwealth countries of which she was then Queen. However, she took her Coronation dress with her on the Commonwealth Tour of 1953 and 1954 and wore it on occasions when she opened Parliaments – in New Zealand, Australia and Ceylon, a somewhat uncomfortable experience since it was very heavy and 'when the sun caught all the diamonte and metalwork embroidery it became so hot that she was burnt, even through all her stiff petticoats.'[72]

Back in Tonga, Queen Salote confessed that she worried that she had upstaged the Queen. She explained: 'I was in a procession headed by Queen Elizabeth who was in a closed coach protected from the rain. Tongans, in such circumstances would never cover their carriage, no matter how wet or cold they may be. In London I was a Tongan so I behaved in our correct and traditional way.'

When asked about the Sultan, she added: 'Yes, I did feel sorry for him. He asked me to close the roof, but I told him I did not understand him. So we continued without any covering.'[73] The memory of Queen Salote remains to this day one of the most popular features of the coronation.

Crown Prince Akihito returned to Tokyo, impressed by the 'solemn dignity and magnificent pageantry of the coronation. At a Japan-British dinner he said: 'Above all the relation between the Royal Family and the nation and the splendid traditional attitude of the British people sank deep into my mind. It is a hard task to digest and make my own all these personal experiences.'[74]

The Crown Prince became Emperor Akihito in 1989. In earlier times Emperors of Japan rarely travelled overseas. When Emperors were appointed to the Order of the Garter, there were Garter Missions as a British Royal Prince made the sea voyage to Japan to bestow the Order. But times have moved on. In 2012 the Emperor thought nothing of flying in to lunch with the Queen and other monarchs in celebration of her Diamond Jubilee.

Richard Dimbleby continued to be the voice of the BBC. When he was dying of cancer in 1965, the Queen sent a footman to the hospital with six bottles of champagne. His memorial service in Westminster Abbey was broadcast live to 5,000,000 people and another 6,500,000 tuned in to watch the recording later in the day.

Many years later James Lees-Milne's diaries revealed that the Duchess of Norfolk had an affair with the Duke of Beaufort, Master of the Horse, a key figure riding in and overseeing the outdoor Coronation processions.[75] At some point in the 1950s, being keen on hunting, she rented a house on the Badminton estate. Whatever the circumstances, the Dukes of Norfolk and Beaufort were civil to each other in public. For many years they walked side by side in the annual procession of the Knights of the Garter. Both men were given the Royal Victorian Chain in the Coronation Honours List.

Fifty years later, on 2 June 2003, the Queen attended a Service of Thanksgiving in Westminster Abbey and paused in the Mall on her way home to unveil a Jubilee Walkway panel. As Chairman of the Jubilee Walkway Trust, I was delighted that she was with us at exactly 12.37 pm, the very moment of crowning fifty years before. I said so in my short speech.

A special 60th anniversary service for the Coronation took place on Tuesday 4 June 2013. For that occasion St Edward's Crown was brought from the Tower of London and placed on the High Altar.

* * * * *

On that wet day in June 1953, Britain acquired a newly anointed and crowned Queen. It is said that the monarch goes into the Abbey as one person and comes out as another. The service was intensely moving for the Queen. After the long procession back through London and the balcony appearances, she could be sure that she had the affirmation and support of the British people and those in the wider Commonwealth, and that she was truly Queen of England and the United Kingdom and all her other realms and territories.

The Queen reigned over Britain for seventy years, celebrating her Diamond Jubilee in 2012, and her Platinum Jubilee in 2022. The young Queen lived to see men walk on the moon, the creation of the Internet and unimaginable changes in the political life of Britain and the Commonwealth. A young mother, she became a grandmother and a great-grandmother. She lived longer than any other British monarch and outreigned Queen Victoria in September 2015. Arguably, she was the world's longest ever reigning monarch, since the record-holder Louis XIV reigned under a Regency until he was thirteen.

The Coronation of King Charles III cannot hope to match the magnificence of the 1953 Coronation, but he will surely succeed to balance the ancient traditions of the service with the diversity of modern Britain.

Appendix

THE REGALIA PEERS

ST EDWARD'S STAFF
3RD EARL OF ANCASTER, TD (1907-83)

Lord Ancaster had served as Lord Great Chamberlain in the last years of George VI's reign from 1951 to 1953. When his father retired, he was called to the House of Lords as Lord Willoughby de Eresby. Previously he had been an MP and from 1933 to 1935 was 'Baby of the House', the youngest sitting MP. Lord Ancaster was also Lord Lieutenant of Lincolnshire. In 1933 he married Phyllis Astor, daughter of Viscount Astor and his wife, Nancy.

Some say that St Edward's Staff was made to guide the footsteps of the monarch, others that its purpose is vague. It is a rod of gold, divided by collars of ornamental leaf patterns (4ft 7 inches long). It is tipped with a steel pike (4¼ inches long) and topped with a mound cross patée. The Sovereign was never invested with this.

THE SCEPTRE WITH THE CROSS
MARSHAL OF THE RAF 1ST VISCOUNT PORTAL OF HUNGERFORD, KG, GCB, OM, DSO, MC (1893-1971)

Lord Portal served as Chief of the Air Staff during World War II. In World War I he served in the Royal Engineers before transferring to the Royal Flying Corps. In April 1940 he was appointed Commander-in-Chief, Bomber Command, and ordered the bombing of Berlin. That October he was appointed Chief of the Air Staff. He did much to improve bombing strategy and accuracy. He was a firm believer that by bombing German cities the morale of the Germans would be undermined. At the coronation he chose to wear the robes of the Order of the Garter, rather than those of a Viscount.

The Sovereign's Royal Sceptre with the Cross is 36 ½ inches long and made of gold with enamel and gems. Six enamelled curves at the top contain the fabulous drop-shaped First Star of Africa diamond – Cullinan I (put there in 1911). Above this is the amethyst orb, surrounded by a jewelled band and topped with an arch of gold, rubies, and diamonds. And above that is the cross patée, thickly set with diamonds, and with a large emerald being in the centre. This sceptre was placed into the Queen's right hand at the coronation.

THE GOLDEN SPURS
21ST BARON HASTINGS (1882-1956) & 4TH BARON CHURSTON (1910-91)

Lord Hastings had carried one of the Golden Spurs at the coronation in 1937. He did this by hereditary right as a direct descendant of Sir John de Hastings, 1st Baron Hastings (1262-1313), whose collateral ancestor, John Marshal, had borne the spurs at the coronation of Richard I in 1189. Lord Hastings lived at Melton Constable, Norfolk (later used as a location in the film, *The Go-Between*).

Lord Churston bore the other spur by the same right of descent as Lord Hastings, in his case through his grandmother, Hon Barbara Yelverton. He too had carried the spurs at the coronation in 1937, when he was 27 years old. Lord Churston served in World War II in the RNVR.

There was some discussion as to whether it was appropriate to present spurs at the coronation of a female sovereign, since they were made to signify the military role of the king. The Queen was clearly not going to wear them. The Spurs are solid gold, richly chased in flowing patterns, and have straps of crimson velvet embroidered in gold. After presentation these spurs are placed on the altar.

THE POINTED SWORD OF JUSTICE TO THE TEMPORALITY
(OR THIRD SWORD)

8TH DUKE OF BUCCLEUCH & (10TH DUKE OF) QUEENSBERRY, PC, KT, GCVO
(1894-1973)

The Duke of Buccleuch was a rich Scottish aristocrat, whose seats included Drumlanrig and Bowhill in Scotland and Boughton House in Northamptonshire. He had been Lord Steward of the Household from 1937 to 1940, but was quietly removed from office for perceived German sympathies. After the war he was restored to royal favour, became Captain-General of the Royal Company of Archers and Gold Stick for Scotland. His sister Alice was married to HRH The Duke of Gloucester. The Duchess of Buccleuch was one of the four duchesses who had held the canopy over Queen Elizabeth at the 1937 coronation despite the fact that the two ladies shared a mutual antipathy for one another, due to both having been courted by Lord Stuart of Findhorn, unfortunately at more or less the same time. The Duke wore his Thistle collar. He had been appointed a Knight of the Thistle by the King in 1949 and installed by the Queen on her visit to Edinburgh in 1952.

The Pointed Sword of Justice to the Temporality is the third of five swords to be found in the Tower of London, and sometimes called the Pointed Sword of Justice. It is steel, silver gilt and gilt iron.

THE POINTED SWORD OF JUSTICE TO THE SPIRITUALITY
(OR SECOND SWORD)
14TH EARL OF HOME, PC (1903-95)

Lord Home is better remembered as Sir Alec Douglas-Home, Conservative Prime Minister from 1963 to 1964. As a young man he played first class cricket. He became an MP in 1931 and served as Neville Chamberlain's Private Secretary. He lost his seat in 1945, regained it in 1950, but went to the House of Lords on inheriting his father's Earldom in 1951. He went on to hold high government office – variously Leader of the House of Lords, Lord President of the Council and he was Foreign Secretary before becoming Prime Minister, and again between 1970 and 1974. In later life he returned to the Lords as Lord Home of the Hirsel. He was appointed a Knight of the Thistle in 1962.

The Pointed Sword of Justice to the Spirituality is the second sword, sometimes called the Sword of Spiritual Justice. Like the Sword of Temporal Justice it is steel, silver gilt and gilt iron.

CURTANA, SWORD OF MERCY
10TH DUKE OF NORTHUMBERLAND (1914-88)

The Duke of Northumberland was the son of Helen, Duchess of Northumberland, Mistress of the Robes to Queen Elizabeth The Queen Mother. He had been a Lord-in-Waiting to George VI and served as Gold Stick-in-Waiting at the 1937 coronation. His wife, Lady Elizabeth Percy, was a daughter of the 8th Duke of Buccleuch. In 1959 he was appointed a Knight of the Garter. He was Lord Lieutenant of Northumberland from 1956 to 1984, and Lord Steward of the Household from 1973 to 1988. By hereditary right, the Dukes of Northumberland are buried in Westminster Abbey.

Curtana, Sword of Mercy is the most curious of the swords, also known as the sword of Edward the Confessor. It has a blunted point to represent the quality of mercy.

THE ROD WITH THE DOVE
9TH DUKE OF RICHMOND & (4TH DUKE OF) GORDON (1904-89)

The Duke of Richmond was a descendant of Charles II and his mistress, Louise de Kérouaille. As a young man he had been a keen racer of motor cars, a member of the Austin team which won Brooklands 500 miles and later with his own team, the Midgets, he won the Brooklands Double Twelve Race. Death duties on inheriting the dukedom in 1935 caused him to sell his Scottish estates and he settled at

Goodwood, near Chichester, where he created the important Goodwood racing circuit in 1948. He had carried the Rod with the Dove at the 1937 coronation.

The Rod with the Dove – or the Sovereign's Sceptre with the Dove, sometimes known as the Rod of Equity and Mercy, is made of gold and 3 feet 7 inches long. An enamelled dove is seated on top of a golden cross, above an orb. Its eyes, beak, and feet are gold. The centre of the sceptre has a band of enamels and gems, and gold openwork with coloured gems, enamels, and diamonds. This sceptre was placed in the Queen's left hand at the Coronation.

THE ORB
FIELD MARSHAL 1ST EARL ALEXANDER OF TUNIS, KG, PC, GCB, GCMG, CSI, DSO, MC (1891-1969)

Lord Alexander of Tunis was one of the great leaders of World War II. He served as GOC-in-C Southern Command from 1940 to 1942, and British Forces in Burma in 1942. He was Commander-in-Chief, Middle East 1942, Deputy C-in-C Allied Forces, North Africa 1943, C-in-C Allied Armies in Italy 1943 to 1944, and Supreme Allied Commander, Mediterranean 1944 to 1945. After the war he was Governor-General and Commander-in-Chief in Canada from 1946 to 1952. At this time he was Minister of Defence (1952 to 1954) and had served on the organising committee for the coronation. Lord Alexander was appointed a Knight of the Garter in 1946 and held numerous important appointments, later being Colonel of Irish Guards, Constable of the Tower of London and Lord Lieutenant of Greater London.

The orb (or the Sovereign's Orb) is gold with enamel and gems and 6 inches in diameter. The cross patée sits on top of a fine amethyst, cut in facets. The orb itself is surrounded by a fillet of gold, outlined by pearls and gems. The orb represents Christ's authority over the globe. The Queen carried it out of the Abbey and it had a special metal arm in the Gold State Coach, so that she could place it there and did not have to hold it during the long procession back to the Palace.

THE SWORD OF STATE
THE 5TH MARQUESS OF SALISBURY, KG (1893-1972).

The jewelled Sword of State is the most important and best known of the swords. It is steel and silver gilt. The scabbard is covered with crimson velvet encircled with gilded metal plates bearing designs in high relief. This sword also appears at the State Opening of Parliament.

ST EDWARD'S CROWN
ADMIRAL OF THE FLEET 1ST VISCOUNT CUNNINGHAM OF HYNDHOPE, KT, GCB, OM, DSO (1883-1963).

The original St Edward's Crown dated back to the reign of Edward the Confessor but was destroyed at the time of the Commonwealth. The current crown was made for Charles II's coronation in 1661. Although it is famously known as the coronation crown it has only been used by a few of Britain's monarchs. Sometimes the crown was carried in procession at other coronations at which it was not actually worn.

The crown is constructed of solid gold, the design including a base with four crosses patée, alternating with four fleurs-de-lis, within which is a velvet cap with ermine border and two arches above, the whole surmounted by a cross, all set with 444 precious stones. Some of the jewels were hired for particular coronations and then detached, leaving only the frame. However, in 1911 the jewels were set permanently into the crown.

George V was the first monarch to be crowned with St Edward's Crown for over 200 years. Queen Victoria and her son, Edward VII chose to be crowned with the lighter Imperial State Crown because St Edward's Crown weighed 4lb 12oz (2.2 kg). St Edward's Crown was placed on the coffin of Edward VII for his lying-in-state and funeral in 1910. Anne Boleyn was crowned with the St Edward's crown at Westminster Abbey on 1 June 1533.

There were various other important pieces of Regalia which were carried in procession:

THE PATEN
RT HON & RT REV WILLIAM WAND, 112TH BISHOP OF LONDON
(1885-1977).

Wand had been Bishop of London, one of the three senior Bishops, since 1945. Before that he had served as Archbishop of Brisbane in Australia before returning to England to be Bishop of Bath and Wells. He was known for his scholarship, skill in administration and unsentimental piety. He was Prelate of the Order of the British Empire.

The Paten (a small plate for the eucharist bread) was also made for Charles II, this time by Robert Vyner's uncle, Thomas. It was used during the Communion part of the service. It was made of gold, probably from the Gold Coast. At rehearsals the Bishop carried the Paten clutched to his chest.

THE CHALICE
RT REV ALWYN WILLIAMS, 92ND BISHOP OF WINCHESTER (1888-1968).

Williams had been Bishop of Winchester since 1952. Before that he was Bishop of Durham. He was a former Headmaster of Winchester College, and chaired the committee that created the New English Bible. By tradition the Bishop of Winchester is Prelate of the Order of the Garter. He was formerly a chaplain to George V.

The Chalice was also made by Thomas Vyner and was used during the communion. It was made of gold like the Paten.

THE BIBLE
RT REV PERCY HERBERT, 67TH BISHOP OF NORWICH (1885-1968)

Herbert had been Bishop of Norwich since 1942. He was a grandson of 2nd Earl of Powis, and was Bishop of Blackburn from 1927 to 1942. After he retired in

1959, he became Rector of St Mary Magdalene's Church at Sandringham and in that role baptised Diana Spencer, future Princess of Wales, in 1961. He served as Clerk of the Closet from 1942 to 1963.

The Bible was obviously not part of the Crown Jewels or Regalia. Oxford University Press printed a special bible for the service. It was then used by the Archbishop when he administered the oath. The bible was then formally presented to the Queen and later placed in the library of Lambeth Palace.

The Imperial State Crown was placed in St Edward's Chapel for the Queen to wear when she processed out of the Abbey. It takes no part in the actual ceremony. This crown was used to crown Queen Victoria and Edward VII. It is the finest crown in the world, containing the Black Prince's Ruby, the Stuart Sapphire (now at the back), the second largest Cullinan Diamond, St Edward's sapphire (worn in his ring by that monarch) and pearls described as Elizabeth I's earrings. This crown had been rebuilt for George VI and the arches were dropped by an inch for the Queen.

Acknowledgements

This is an updated edition of the book *Coronation*, which I wrote in 2013. I am too young to remember the coronation. I am just a Georgian, having been born a few weeks before the King George VI died. On coronation day I was in my pram on the balcony of our then flat in Egerton Gardens in London – or so I was told. I guess the hood of the pram was firmly up. Meanwhile my parents and their friends gathered in front of the television set, bought as in so many homes across Britain, specially for this occasion. I did sit through the entire coronation service on 1 January 1977 when the BBC re-showed the seven hour live coverage, minute for minute. By the end of it, I felt I knew many of the key figures as they went through their paces in the Abbey. It was a wonderful thing to have seen.

Since then I have studied the ceremony in great detail, delving into the Cabinet papers and Foreign Office papers at the National Archives, Archbishop Fisher's papers at Lambeth Palace and further papers in the library of Westminster Abbey. Some years ago I acquired a cache of private papers mainly relating to the 1937 coronation, which proved fascinating. I also bought the privately printed volumes relating to the coronations of Edward VII and George V, and the Records of Summonses, Invitations and Seatings to the Coronations of George VI and Elizabeth II.

While writing this book, I particularly enjoyed a day long seminar on the coronation by the historian, David Thomas, at St George's School, Windsor, on 22 February 2013. I am grateful to many for information, in particular Sir Roy Strong, Hon James Stourton, Patric Dickinson (former Clarenceux King of Arms), John Martin Robinson (Maltravers Herald Extraordinary), Caroline Knox, John Murray, Tim O'Donovan, Michael Pick and Bruce Anderson.

Notes

ACCESSION

1 T.C. Banks, *An Historical and Critical Enquiry into the Nature of the Kingly Office* (Sherwood, Neely and Jones, 1814), p. x.

2 C.E. Vulliamy, *Royal George* (Jonathan Cape, 1937), p. 72.

3 Frank Bardon, *Sensation at the Coronation* (miscellaneous press cutting, ca. 1936).

4 *The Coronation Book of Queen Elizabeth II* (Odhams Press, 1953), p. 29 – A.L. Rowse quoting Horace Walpole.

5 T.C. Banks, *An Historical and Critical Enquiry into the Nature of the Kingly Office* (Sherwood, Neely and Jones, 1814), p. xv.

6 T.C. Banks, *An Historical and Critical Enquiry into the Nature of the Kingly Office* (Sherwood, Neely and Jones, 1814), p. xvi.

7 Christopher Hibbert, *George IV – Regent & King* (Allen Lane, 1973), p. 192.

8 The Times, 29 June 1838; & 29 May 1953.

9 Charles Greville (ed), *A Journal of the Reign of Queen Victoria, Volume I* – 1837-1852 (D. Appleton, 1885), p. 106.

10 HRH The Duke of Windsor, *The Crown & The People* 1902-1953 (Cassell, 1953), p. 14.

11 Sarah Bradford, *George VI* (Weidenfeld & Nicolson, 1989), p. 214.

12 Sir Osbert Sitwell to Cecil Beaton, quoted in Cecil Beaton's unpublished diary, 12 May 1937.

13 Cecil Beaton, unpublished diary, 12 May 1937 [St John's College, Cambridge].

14 Rt Revd Herbert Hensley Henson, *Retrospect from an Unimportant Life, Volume II* (Oxford University Press, 1943), p. 383.

15 10th Duke of Argyll to Revd Bartholomew Hack, May 1937 [author's private collection].

16 William Shawcross, *Queen and Country* (BBC, 2002), p. 49.

17 Sir William R. Anson, *The Law and Custom of the Constitution* (Clarendon Press, 1897), pp. 227-8.

18 T.C. Banks, *An Historical and Critical Enquiry into the Nature of the Kingly Office* (Sherwood, Neely and Jones, 1814), p. ix.

19 *The Times*, 5 November 1952.

PREPARATION

1 *The Times*, 5 May 1953.

2 Caroline Elliot (ed), *The BBC Book of Royal Memories* (BBC Books, 1991), p. 39.

3 Derived from James Wilkinson, *The Queen's Coronation* (Scala Publications, 2011), p. 31.

4 Leonard Miall (ed), *Richard Dimbleby – Broadcaster* (BBC, 1966), p. 79.

5 The Earl Marshal's Press Conference at Church House, 3 March 1953 – PREM 11/34 (National Archives).

6 *Daily Telegraph*, 2 April 2015

7 James Lees-Milne, *Ancestral Voices* (Chatto & Windus, 1975), p. 230

8 The Duke of Norfolk to Lord Woolton, 5 January 1953, quoted in The Earl of Woolton, *The Memoirs of the Rt Hon the Earl of Woolton* (Cassell, 1959), p. 385.

9 Coronation notes of Garter King of Arms, 1936-7, including correspondence dated 30 October 1936 (in the possession of the author).

10 *The Times*, 1 November 1952.

11 CAB 128/25 – CC 52 60 – 17 June 1952 (National Archives).

12 *The Times*, 2 August 1952.

13 Very Rev Alan Don, *The Coronation* – 63189 (Westminster Abbey Archives).

14 *Dictionary of National Biography* 1971-81 (Oxford University Press, 1986), p. 316.

15 *Dictionary of National Biography* 1971-81 (Oxford University Press, 1986), p. 317.

16 C.L. Sulzberger, *A Long Row of Candles* (The Macmillan Company, Canada, 1969), p. 880.

17 *The Times*, 5 May 1952.

18 Edward Carpenter, *Archbishop Fisher – His Life and Times* (The Canterbury Press, 1991), p. 251.

19 *The Times*, 3 October 1952.

20 Edward Carpenter, *Archbishop Fisher – His Life and Times* (The Canterbury Press, 1991), p. 266.

21 The Archbishop of Canterbury to Very Rev Alan Don, 25 July 1952. (Westminster Abbey Archives).

22 E.C. Ratcliff, *The Coronation Service* (SPCK, 1953), p. 23).

23 E.C. Ratcliff, *The Coronation Service* (SPCK, 1953), p. 14.

24 E.C. Ratcliff Memorandum on the Revision of the Coronation Service, 13 June 1952, pp. 2-3 (63258) (Westminster Abbey Archives).

25 E.C. Ratcliff Memorandum on the Revision of the Coronation Service, 13 June 1952, p. 15 (63258) (Westminster Abbey Archives).

26 Archbishop Fisher's coronation diary, 6 November 1952 (Lambeth Palace Library).

27 Archbishop Fisher's coronation diary, 6 November 1952 (Lambeth Palace Library).

28 Lawrence Tanner notes on Dr Ratcliff's Memorandum on the Revision of the Coronation Service – September 1952 (63260 B) (Westminster Abbey Archives).

29 *The Times*, 18 March 1953.

30 *The Times*, 19 March 1953.

31 Very Alan Don to the Archbishop of Canterbury, 18 February 1953 (63270); & Archbishop of Canterbury to Very Rev Alan Don, 18 February 1953 (63268) (Westminster Abbey Archives).

32 The Archbishop of Canterbury, *I Here Present Unto You...* (SPCK, 1953), p. 14.

33 James Wilkinson, *Westminster Abbey – 1,000 Years of Music and Pageant* (Westminster Abbey Archives).

34 John Colville to Rt Hon Winston Churchill, 7 July 1952 – PREM 11/34 (National Archives).

35 CAB 128/24 – CC 52 67 – 10 July 1952 (National Archives).

36 Ven F.H. House to Very Rev Alan Don, 28 July 1952 (Westminster Abbey Archives).

37 The Duke of Norfolk to Very Rev Alan Don, 4 August 1952 (Westminster Abbey Archives).

38 *Daily Telegraph*, 24 October 1952.

39 Norman Brook, Memorandum: Coronation: Television – 24 October 1952 – PREM 11/34 (National Archives).

40 CAB 128/52 CC 52 90 – 28 October 1952; & CAB 129/56 CC 52 367 – 27 October 1952 (National Archives).

41 The Archbishop of Canterbury to Ven Francis House, 24 February 1953 (Lambeth Palace Library).

42 *Sunday Telegraph,* 9 January 1983.

43 CAB 128/26 – CC 53 02 – 10 February 1953 (National Archives).

44 *The Times*, 25 October 1952.

45 CAB 128/25 – CC 52 96 – 13 November 1952 (National Archives).

46 *The Times*, 27 December 1952.

47 *The Times*, 29 December 1952.

48 *The Times*, 9 January 1953.

49 Sir Claud Schuster to Garter King of Arms, Lord Chancellor's Office, House of Lords, 24 November 1936 (Coronation notes of Garter King of Arms, 1936-7 – in the possession of the author).

50 Nigel Starck, *Life After Death: The Art of the Obituary* (Melbourne University Publishing, 2006), p. 90; *Daily Telegraph* obituary, April 1988.

51 *The Times*, 16 April 1953.

52 HRH The Duke of Windsor, *The Crown and the People* 1902-1953 (Cassell,

1953), p. 7.

53 *The Times*, 3 December 1952.

54 James Wilkinson, *The Queen's Coronation* (Scala Publishers, 2011), p. 23.

55 Hugo Vickers, *Alice, Princess Andrew of Greece* (Hamish Hamilton, 2000), p. 347.

56 Hugo Vickers, *Alice, Princess Andrew of Greece* (Hamish Hamilton, 2000), p. 348.

57 Hugo Vickers, *Alice, Princess Andrew of Greece* (Hamish Hamilton, 2000), p. 348.

56 His Royal Highness Prince Chula Chakrabongse of Thailand, *The Twain Have Met* (Foulis & Co, 1956), p. 285.

58 Count Hans Veit Toerring to author, quoted in HRH The Duke of Kent & Hugo Vickers, *A Royal Life* (Hodder & Stoughton, 2022), p. 129

59 J. A. Pilcher to R. H. Scott, Foreign Office, 29 October 1952 – JAPAN FO 371 99 533 1952 – (National Archives).

60 Sir Esla Dening to Rt Hon Anthony Eden, 17 December 1952 – JAPAN FO 371 99 533 1952 (National Archives).

61 Sir Esla Dening to Rt Hon Anthony Eden, 17 December 1952 – JAPAN FO 371 99 533 1952 (National Archives).

62 The Earl of Swinton to the Archbishop of Canterbury, 22 January 1953 (Lambeth Palace Library).

63 *The Times*, 21 May 1953.

64 Archbishop Fisher's coronation diary, 6 November 1952 (Lambeth Palace Library).

65 Hugo Vickers, *Behind Closed Doors* (Hutchinson, 2011), p. 347.

66 *The Times*, 17 December 1952.

67 23B FO/371 97 137 – 6 November 1952 (National Archives).

68 23B FO/371 97 137 – 6 November 1952 (National Archives).

69 FO/371 102959 (National Archives).

70 Oliver Warner, *Cunningham of Hyndhope* (John Murray, 1967), p. 279.

71 Private information.

72 *Dictionary of National Biography,* 1961-1970 (Oxford University Press, 1981), p. 249.

73 Robert Rhodes James (ed), *Chips – The Diaries of Sir Henry Channon* (Weidenfeld & Nicolson, 1967), p. 476.

74 Obituary of 6th Marquess of Cholmondeley, by Hugo Vickers, *The Independent*, 16 March 1990.

75 Anne Glenconner, *Lady in Waiting* (Hodder & Stoughton, 2019), p. 61.

76 Anne Glenconner, *Lady in Waiting* (Hodder & Stoughton, 2019), p. 61.

77 Private note by Lord Hardinge of Penshurst, quoted in Hugo Vickers, *Royal Orders* (Boxtree, 1994), p. 56n.

78 Cecil Beaton, diary 31 May 1953, quoted in Hugo Vickers, *Cecil Beaton*

(Weidenfeld & Nicolson, 1985), p. 367.

79 Michael Bloch (ed), *James Lees-Milne Diaries* 1942-1954 (John Murray, 2006), p. 452.

80 *The Times*, 15 January 1953.

81 *The Times*, 19 January 1953.

82 Norman Hartnell, *Silver and Gold* (Evans Brothers, 1955), p. 124.

83 Norman Hartnell, *Silver and Gold* (Evans Brothers, 1955), p. 124.

84 Andrew Barrow, *Gossip* (Hamish Hamilton, 1978), p. 174.

85 Norman Hartnell, *Silver and Gold* (Evans Brothers, 1955), p. 129.

86 *Daily Sketch*, 2 June 1953.

87 Norman Hartnell, *Silver and Gold* (Evans Brothers, 1955), p. 134.

88 Hon Margaret Wyndham to James Pope-Hennessy, August 1956 (Sir John Pope-Hennessy papers, Getty Museum, Los Angeles).

89 Queen Elizabeth The Queen Mother to Sir Arthur Penn, 12 April 1953 (quoted in William Shawcross, *Queen Elizabeth The Queen Mother* (Macmillan,2009), p.677.

90 Caroline Elliot (ed), *The BBC Book of Royal Memories* (BBC Books, 1991), p. 40.

91 *The Coronation and the BBC* (BBC, 1953), p. 8.

92 *The Times,* 12 May 1953.

93 Hugo Vickers, *The Royal Mews* (Royal Collection Enterprises, 2002), p. 31.

94 *The Times,* 12 May 1953.

95 Winston S. Churchill, *Memories and Adventures* (Weidenfeld & Nicolson, 1989), p. 76.

96 Winston S. Churchill, *Memories and Adventures* (Weidenfeld & Nicolson, 1989), p. 76.

97 Coronation of Her Majesty Queen Elizabeth II – Westminster Abbey 2nd June 1953- Ceremonial Detail: Notes and Plans (Garter King of Arms's confidential copy – in the possession of the author), p. 3.

98 Coronation of Her Majesty Queen Elizabeth II – Westminster Abbey 2nd June 1953 - Ceremonial Detail: Notes and Plans, Map 40 – in the possession of the author.

99 Archbishop Fisher's coronation diary (Lambeth Palace Library).

100 Archbishop Fisher to HRH The Duke of Edinburgh, 22 May 1953 (copy in Lambeth Palace Library).

101 *Westminster Abbey Chorister,* 1993 (Westminster Abbey Archives).

102 Very Rev Alan Don, *The Coronation* – 63189 (Westminster Abbey Archives).

103 Osbert Lancaster, *Studies from the Life* (Gryphon Books, 1954), p. 43.

104 Archbishop Fisher's coronation diary (Lambeth Palace Library).

105 Edward Carpenter, *Archbishop Fisher – His Life and Times* (The Canterbury Press, 1991), p. 262.

106 Archbishop Fisher's coronation diary (Lambeth Palace Library).

107 Archbishop Fisher's coronation diary (Lambeth Palace Library).

108 Garter King of Arms to the Archbishop of Canterbury, 24 May 1953 (Lambeth Palace Library).

109 Archbishop Fisher's coronation diary (Lambeth Palace Library).

110 Garter King of Arms to the Archbishop of Canterbury, 24 May 1953 (Lambeth Palace Library).

111 Archbishop Fisher's coronation diary (Lambeth Palace Library).

112 Archbishop Fisher's coronation diary (Lambeth Palace Library).

113 Michael Bloch (ed), *James Lees-Milne Diaries* 1942-1954 (John Murray, 2006), p. 452.

114 Cecil Beaton, unpublished diary, 31 May 1952 (St John's College, Cambridge).

115 Cecil Beaton, unpublished diary, 31 May 1952 (St John's College, Cambridge).

116 Graham Payn & Sheridan Morley (eds), *The Noël Coward Diaries* (Weidenfeld & Nicolson, 1982), p. 213 – entry for 24 May 1953.

117 *Household Brigade Magazine, Coronation Number*, 1953, p.99.

118 *Daily Sketch*, 1 June 1953.

119 Osbert Lancaster, *Studies from the Life* (Gryphon Books, 1954), p. 44.

120 Archbishop Fisher's coronation diary (Lambeth Palace Library).

121 Andrew Barrow, *Gossip* (Hamish Hamilton, 1978), p. 174.

122 Lady Diana Cooper to Patrick Leigh Fermor, 15 June 1953, quoted in Philip Ziegler, *Diana Cooper* (Hamish Hamilton, 1981), p. 276.

CORONATION DAY

1 *Household Brigade Magazine, Coronation Number*, 1953, p.101.

2 Jonathan Dimbleby, *Richard Dimbleby* (Hodder & Stoughton, 1975), p. 243.

3 Cecil Beaton, unpublished diary, 31 May 1952 (St John's College, Cambridge).

4 *The Times*, 2 June 1953.

5 Princess Alice, Countess of Athlone, *For My Grandchildren* (Evans Brothers, 1966), p. 286.

6 *The Memoirs of Princess Alice, Duchess of Gloucester* (Collins, 1983), p. 175.

7 Robert Rhodes James (ed), *Chips, the Diaries of Sir Henry Channon* (Weidenfeld & Nicolson, 1967), p. 475.

8 C.L. Sulzberger, *A Long Row of Candles* (The Macmillan Company, Canada, 1969), p. 878.

9 Robert Rhodes James (ed), *Chips, the Diaries of Sir Henry Channon* (Weidenfeld & Nicolson, 1967), pp. 475.

10 Lady Diana Cooper to Patrick Leigh Fermor, 15 June 1953, quoted in Frank &

Anita Kermode (ed), *The Oxford Book of Letters* (Oxford University Press), p. 528.

11 Iain Tennant, *One Thing After Another* (privately printed at M & N Print, 1990), p. 208.

12 Iain Tennant, *One Thing After Another* (privately printed at M & N Print, 1990), p. 207.

13 Robert Rhodes James (ed), *Chips, the Diaries of Sir Henry Channon* (Weidenfeld & Nicolson, 1967), pp. 475-6.

14 Cecil Beaton, unpublished diary, 31 May 1952 (St John's College, Cambridge).

15 Robert Rhodes James (ed), *Chips, the Diaries of Sir Henry Channon* (Weidenfeld & Nicolson, 1967), pp. 476.

16 Cecil Beaton, unpublished diary, 31 May 1952 (St John's College, Cambridge).

17 Lady Diana Cooper to Patrick Leigh Fermor, 15 June 1953, quoted in Frank & Anita Kermode (ed), *The Oxford Book of Letters* (Oxford University Press), p. 528.

18 Robert Rhodes James (ed), *Chips, the Diaries of Sir Henry Channon* (Weidenfeld & Nicolson, 1967), pp. 476.

19 Lady Diana Cooper to Patrick Leigh Fermor, 15 June 1953, quoted in Frank & Anita Kermode (ed), *The Oxford Book of Letters* (Oxford University Press), p. 529.

20 Cecil Beaton, unpublished diary, 31 May 1952 (St John's College, Cambridge).

21 Lady Diana Cooper to Patrick Leigh Fermor, 15 June 1953, quoted in Frank & Anita Kermode (ed), *The Oxford Book of Letters* (Oxford University Press), pp. 528-9.

22 Cecil Beaton, unpublished diary, 31 May 1952 (St John's College, Cambridge).

23 Very Rev Alan Don, *The Coronation* – 63189 (Westminster Abbey Archives).

24 Very Rev Alan Don, *The Coronation* – 63189 (Westminster Abbey Archives).

25 Oliver Warner, *Cunningham of Hyndhope* (John Murray, 1967), p. 266.

26 Archbishop Fisher's notes on the coronation (Lambeth Palace Library).

27 Michael Bloch (ed), *James Lees-Milne Diaries* 1942-1954 (John Murray, 2006), p. 453.

28 L.E. Tanner, *Recollections of a Westminster Antiquary*, p. 152 (Westminster Abbey Archives).

29 L.E. Tanner, *Recollections of a Westminster Antiquary*, p. 152 (Westminster Abbey Archives).

30 Very Rev Alan Don, *The Coronation* – 63189 (Westminster Abbey Archives).

31 Robert Rhodes James (ed), *Chips, the Diaries of Sir Henry Channon* (Weidenfeld & Nicolson, 1967), pp. 476.

32 *Country Life Coronation Number*, June 1953, p. 33.

33 L. G. Wickham Legg, *English Coronation Records* (Constable, 1901), p. 25.

34 Jonathan Dimbleby, *The Prince of Wales* (Little, Brown, 1994), p. 204

35 *Country Life Coronation Number*, June 1953, pp. 33-4.

36 Archbishop Fisher's notes on the coronation (Lambeth Palace Library).

37 Very Rev Alan Don, *The Coronation* – 63189 (Westminster Abbey Archives).

38 Edward Carpenter, *Archbishop Fisher – His Life and Times* (The Canterbury Press, 1991), p. 263.

39 Archbishop Fisher's notes on the coronation (Lambeth Palace Library).

40 C.L. Sulzberger, *A Long Row of Candles* (The Macmillan Company, Canada, 1969), p. 878.

41 Audrey Russell, *A Certain Voice* (Ross Anderson Publications, 1989), p. 102.

42 Winston S. Churchill, *Memories and Adventures* (Weidenfeld & Nicolson, 1989), p. 76.

43 L.E. Tanner, *Recollections of a Westminster Antiquary*, p. 152 (Westminster Abbey Archives).

44 Private Information.

45 Lady Diana Cooper to Patrick Leigh Fermor, 15 June 1953, quoted in Frank & Anita Kermode (ed), *The Oxford Book of Letters* (Oxford University Press), p. 529.

46 Archbishop Fisher's notes on the coronation (Lambeth Palace Library).

47 Edward Carpenter, *Archbishop Fisher – His Life and Times* (The Canterbury Press, 1991), p. 263.

48 Anthony Garnett, *Coronation* (printed note in Westminster Abbey Archives).

49 Princess Alice, Countess of Athlone, *For My Grandchildren* (Evans Brothers, 1966), p. 287.

50 Archbishop Fisher's notes on the coronation (Lambeth Palace Library).

51 Archbishop Fisher's notes on the coronation (Lambeth Palace Library).

52 Very Rev Alan Don, *The Coronation* – 63189 (Westminster Abbey Archives).

53 Very Rev Alan Don, *The Coronation* – 63189 (Westminster Abbey Archives).

54 HRH The Duke of Kent to author, quoted in HRH The Duke of Kent & Hugo Vickers, *A Royal Life* (Hodder & Stoughton, 2022), p. 125.

55 HRH Prince Michael of Kent to author, quoted in HRH The Duke of Kent & Hugo Vickers, *A Royal Life* (Hodder & Stoughton, 2022), p. 128.

56 Harold Macmillan diary, 1-7 June 1953, quoted in Peter Caterall (ed), *The Macmillan Diaries, 1950-1957* (Macmillan, 2003), p. 235.

57 Lady Diana Cooper to Patrick Leigh Fermor, 15 June 1953, quoted in Frank & Anita Kermode (ed), *The Oxford Book of Letters* (Oxford University Press), p. 529.

58 Robert Rhodes James (ed), *Chips, the Diaries of Sir Henry Channon* (Weidenfeld & Nicolson, 1967), pp. 477.

59 Sir Harry Luke, *Queen Salote and her Kingdom* (Putnam, 1954), pp. 115-6.

60 Michael Bloch (ed), *James Lees-Milne Diaries 1942-1954* (John Murray, 2006), p. 453.

61 *The Memoirs of Princess Alice, Duchess of Gloucester* (Collins, 1983), p. 175.

62 Private Information.

63 The Duke of Norfolk to the Archbishop of Canterbury, 24 April 1953 (Lambeth Palace Library).

64 Martin Gilbert, *Winston S. Churchill, Volume VIII – 'Never Despair'* (Heinemann, 1988), p.836.

65 *The Guardian*, 3 June 1953.

66 *The Times*, 5 June 1953.

65 Osbert Lancaster, *Studies from the Life* (Gryphon Books, 1954), p. 43.

67 The Archbishop of Canterbury to George Barnes, 9 June 1953 (Lambeth Palace Library).

68 The Archbishop of Canterbury to the Duke of Norfolk, 10 June 1953 (Lambeth Palace Library).

70 The Queen to the Archbishop of Canterbury, 20 June 1953, quoted in Edward Carpenter, *Archbishop Fisher – His Life and Times* (The Canterbury Press, 1991), p. 264.

71 *The Times*, 6 June 1953.

72 Pamela Hicks, *Daughter of Empire* (Weidenfeld & Nicolson, 2012), p. 248.

73 Nelson Eustis, *The King of Tonga* (Hyde Park Press, Adelaide, Australia, 1997), pp. 84-5.

74 *The Times*, 18 December 1953.

75 Michael Bloch (ed), *Holy Dread* (James Lees-Milne Diaries 1982-1984), p. 204.